HISTORICAL REDRESS

THINK NOW

Think Now is a new series of books which examines central contemporary social and political issues from a philosophical perspective. These books aim to be accessible, rather than overly technical, bringing philosophical rigour to modern questions which matter the most to us. Provocative yet engaging, the authors take a stand on political and cultural themes of interest to any intelligent reader.

AVAILABLE NOW:

Beyond Animal Rights, Tony Milligan

Ethics of Climate Change, James Garvey

Ethics of Metropolitan Growth, Robert Kirkman

Ethics of Trade and Aid, Christopher D. Wraight

Just Warriors Inc., Deane-Peter Baker

Libertarian Anarchy, Gerard Casey

Nanoethics, Donal P. O'Mathuna

Personal Responsibility, Alexander Brown

Terrorism, Nicholas Fotion

War and Ethics, Nicholas Fotion

SERIES EDITORS:

James Garvey is Secretary of the Royal Institute of Philosophy, UK. He is the author of *The Twenty Greatest Philosophy Books* and *The Ethics of Climate Change*, also published by Continuum.

Jeremy Stangroom is co-editor, with Julian Baggini, of *The Philosophers' Magazine* and co-author of *Why Truth Matters*, *What Philosophers Think* and *Great Thinkers A-Z* (all Continuum)

HISTORICAL REDRESS

Must we pay for the past?

RICHARD VERNON

continuum

Continuum International Publishing Group

The Tower Building   80 Maiden Lane
11 York Road   Suite 704
London   New York
SE1 7NX   NY 10038

www.continuumbooks.com

© Richard Vernon, 2012

All rights reserved. No part of this publication may be reproduced or transmitted in any form or by any means, electronic or mechanical, including photocopying, recording, or any information storage or retrieval system, without prior permission in writing from the publishers.

The Author has asserted his right under the Copyright, Designs and Patents Act, 1988, to be identified as Author of this work.

British Library Cataloguing-in-Publication Data
A catalogue record for this book is available from the British Library.

ISBN: HB: 978-1-4411-6651-7
PB: 978-1-4411-2131-8

Library of Congress Cataloging-in-Publication Data
Vernon, Richard, 1945-
Historical redress : must we pay for the past? / Richard Vernon.
  pages cm. – (Think now)
Includes bibliographical references and index.
ISBN 978-1-4411-2131-8 (pbk. : alk. paper) – ISBN 978-1-4411-6651-7 (hardcover : alk. paper) – ISBN 978-1-4411-5978-6 (ebook epub : alk. paper) – ISBN 978-1-4411-8089-6 (ebook pdf : alk. paper) 1. Reparations for historical injustices–Philosophy. 2. Justice (Philosophy) 3. Responsibility–Philosophy. I. Title.

B105.J87V47 2012
320.01'1–dc23

2011048716

Typeset by Newgen Imaging Systems Pvt Ltd, Chennai, India
Printed and bound in India

CONTENTS

Introduction 1
Let us begin with a list 1

1 Does the past have rights? 17
Why rights matter 19
The testamentary model 21
Our interests survive us 24
Can the dead be harmed? 30
Posthumous rights and cold cases 32
The 'too abstract' objection 36

2 Who benefits? 40
Does anyone benefit? 41
Does injustice pay? 44
Baseline issues 47
Do benefits create duties? 52
Unjust Enrichment 56
Is redress the right response? 61

3 What memory calls for 64
Kinds of memory 67
What truth commissions can do 72
Public apology 80
From apology to identity 86

4 **Because we are who we are** 88
Relationship terms 90
Nation, or state? 94
Complicity 102
Political continuity 104

5 **Back to the future** 111
Inherited wrongs 112
The lynching of Louis Sam 114
Why history matters 116
Ants and grasshoppers 122
On clarity 126

Conclusion 131

Notes 155
Bibliography 167
Index 173

INTRODUCTION

Let us begin with a list

1 In the early 1800s, Lord Elgin, a British diplomat, removed a large quantity of marble sculpture from the Parthenon in Athens – including over 200 feet of very beautiful decorative frieze – and had it shipped back to England. The sculptures were eventually purchased for the British Museum in London, where they are among the Museum's largest and best-known displays. For many years, the government of Greece (supported by public opinion in Greece, and elsewhere[1]) has vigorously demanded their return. Similarly, there are demands in many countries for the return of treasures that were looted by invading armies, from Napoleon's time to the recent past. And in North America, museums face demands – which are often accepted – for the return of artefacts such as religious masks and ceremonial items that were taken from native peoples. In one particularly high-profile case, the famous Smithsonian Institution in Washington, DC, negotiated the return of the remains of a native people's last surviving member, remains that had been stored in its 'anthropological' collection.[2] But even in the 1990s, it was estimated that by some accounts, there were still hundreds of thousands more sets of remains in museums and elsewhere.[3]

2 On a larger scale, aboriginal people (and people of mixed race) in North America, Australasia and South America claim that land seized from them by settlers be returned to their control, or that compensation be made. Some claims relate to treaties that were simply broken, some to treaties that were unfairly interpreted, some to treaties that were made on the basis of fraud or coercion, while some demands relate to seizures or encroachments that were made without any legal basis at all. Often wrapped up in these claims is a more basic demand that white societies acknowledge the wrong of failing to respect native societies' right to be treated as sovereign peoples.

3   Aboriginal people also have grievances relating to their treatment by governments, such as, in Australia, the United States and Canada, the policy of forced assimilation of aboriginal children in Residential Schools. The policy continued for about 100 years, ending only in the later part of the twentieth century. In 2006, the Canadian government reached a settlement establishing various forms of monetary compensation and a 'Truth and Reconciliation Commission' – modelled on similar commissions in South Africa and elsewhere – to establish and publicize the facts about the children's experience. Grievances related to mistreatment are not of course confined to the aboriginal case. In the course of the Second World War, the Japanese compelled thousands of South-East Asian (mainly Korean) women into prostitution.[4] Known euphemistically as 'comfort women', those who survived have pursued a sustained campaign against the Japanese government, aimed at securing compensation and apology, with inconclusive results so far. Meanwhile, Japanese-Americans and Japanese-Canadians have campaigned (successfully) for compensation recognizing their indiscriminate internment, under harsh conditions, by the US and Canadian governments during the Second World War.

4   Behind all such campaigns, there is, of course, the massive example of demands for Holocaust reparations. In the 1950s, the Federal German Republic (the former 'West Germany') transferred over a billion Deutschmarks to Israel, most of it described as funds for the resettlement costs arising from Nazi policies of terror and extermination. Later compensation

payments included, in 2000, payments to about a million former slaves and forced labourers (Jewish and non-Jewish) in central and eastern Europe, the money coming both from the German government and from corporations that had employed forced labour. Swiss banks, complicit in several ways in the Holocaust – by holding German gold reserves that had financed the war, by (effectively) confiscating funds from concentration camp victims – were induced after many years of pressure to establish a fund for compensating the Holocaust victims and their descendants. The Armenians, however, victims of what is generally seen as the first genocide of the twentieth century (in 1915), still seek acknowledgement and apology from the government of Turkey (which apparently takes the view that there was no genocidal intent).

5 The only case that is comparable to the Holocaust or other genocides or to the treatment of aboriginal peoples is, of course, African slavery. In the past few decades, many demands have been made, on many institutions, for reparations. The Aetna Insurance Company faced legal suits and a boycott, after the discovery that it had issued life insurance policies to slave owners covering the lives of their slaves, thus profiting directly from the slave economy. Another institution, Brown University, it turned out, had been founded (under the name of Rhode Island College) with funds derived from the slave trade, and in response to sustained protest, the university eventually agreed to a settlement involving research and teaching in the history of slavery, scholarships for black students, and other items. Various organizations have launched legal suits and political campaigns against the government of the United States itself, some based upon broken promises made to freed slaves during the Civil War, others on the US government's failure to carry out its constitutional obligations in the post–Civil War period, when the repression and exploitation of black people continued despite their legal enfranchisement.

6 Countries with an imperial past are, understandably, often the object of claims for redress. To pick just a few examples from the British case: In 1999, Queen Elizabeth II, on a state visit to South Africa, apologized to 'all South Africans' for violence inflicted in the Boer War a century earlier (disappointing members of the Afrikaner community who had wanted an apology directed specifically at themselves). In 2003, the Queen issued an apology, through the Canadian government, for the expulsion (250 years before) of the Acadians, French-speaking people who refused to swear allegiance to the British Crown, and so were regarded as a security risk in its newly acquired possessions in eastern Canada. (Interestingly, the Acadian community expressly declined to ask for anything beyond an apology, such as reparations.) In 2011, the Queen, during an historic visit to Ireland, made a statement acknowledging and regretting past violence (though without using the word 'apology' itself). Also in 2011, survivors of the British repression of the independence movement in Kenya in the 1950s launched a lawsuit for damages, prompting the release of information about the extent of brutality involved, and an apology from the British Prime Minister.

7 It is not only states, among major institutions, that experience pressure to make redress. The Church of England has recently apologized for its hostile reaction to Charles Darwin's *Origin of Species*. Even more belatedly, the Catholic Church had previously apologized for its persecution of Galileo on account of his heretical views about astronomy. A Polish diocese of the Church has ceremoniously reburied the remains of Copernicus, with apologies for its opposition to his views some 500 years ago. And Pope John Paul II's repeated and eloquent efforts to acknowledge the Church's role in abetting Jewish persecution are often welcomed as a moral breakthrough, given the institution's long history of complicity in anti-Semitism.[5]

INTRODUCTION 5

This list could, of course, be made very much longer. But I hope that even this short list is enough to show that the idea of righting old wrongs is one that is taken very seriously, and in many different contexts, large and smaller. Many more examples of apology and reparation, some of them much less well known than those listed above, are listed and described on an excellent website.[6] The first instance recorded there dates to 1077, but as the website's list shows, it is in the past few decades that the volume of demands for redress, of one kind or another, has increased very sharply. Why this should be so is an interesting question, which some commentators have tried to answer. Focusing on the issue of apologies, one study of press coverage in the United States shows that frequency rose sharply, almost doubling, in the course of the 1990s.[7] No doubt that has something to do with the increasingly multicultural nature of Western societies, in which groups with different histories interact and look for ways to assert their identity. Perhaps it has something to do with a shift away from class-based politics in which demands are made for general equality, allowing space for a politics in which demands based on particular injustices can be made. But this book is not about why historical redress has become so topical, although that is an important subject: It is about the *ethics* of redress, or the reasons that underpin the demands for redress and for resistance to them. There are many such reasons, both for redress and for resistance, as we shall see.

When one person wrongs another, shouldn't the wrong be righted? There are several ways in which we might think about what it means to right it. One way, the standard way in justice systems in Western societies, is punishment: The wrongdoer should suffer a penalty, proportionate in some sense to the wrong he has caused. The wrongdoer, we might say, has implicitly claimed a sort of privilege, acting as though his interest in getting or doing something was more important than his victim's: Punishment imposes some penalty that strikes down this claim to privilege, by damaging an interest of the wrongdoer – typically, his interest in liberty (by imprisonment).[8] The practice of righting wrongs by punishing wrongdoers is well established, of course, in the case of ordinary crime, but in the late twentieth century, an effort was made to extend punishment to the actions of states, and in this way, to respond to some of the wrongs listed above. Developments in international law, especially the creation of criminal courts empowered to punish atrocities that would otherwise have been sheltered by state sovereignty, have been a strikingly novel feature in international affairs in the past few decades. What is meant by *redress*, however, is different in a very fundamental way. Punishment is all about imposing a loss of some kind on the person (or institution) who did wrong. Redress, on the other hand, is all about making up the loss that was suffered by the victim. The point is not to strike at the perpetrators, but to make good the damage that they have caused to victims.

Perhaps the simplest of all the responses to wrongdoing is that the person who was wronged should recover what was taken from him or her. Suppose I take something of yours, let us say your mountain bike: At least an important part of righting that wrong is that I should give it back.[9] I should give it back even if I took it last week. Or last year. Or 10 years ago. You suffered a loss, and there is a really straightforward way to repair it, even though time passes. But suppose we stretch out the time, to, let us say, 50 or 100 years. And suppose it was not me who took the mountain bike from someone, but my father or uncle or great-grandfather. And suppose it was not you who lost the mountain bike, but your mother or aunt or great-grandmother. And suppose the mountain bike does not exist anymore – it has been cannibalized to provide parts for other bikes, or it has been sold for scrap. Who then owes what to whom? The whole thing seems to have become quite a bit more complicated – as *historical* redress almost always is. With the passage of time, we move progressively away from the simplicity of the 'you took it from me so give it back' model.

Complicated or not, though, many policies recently adopted by states clearly express the belief that redress must be made even though the people who actually committed or suffered the wrong are now departed, and even though what was originally taken is no longer in a returnable state. Or, a further complication, perhaps it was never a returnable kind of thing to begin with – perhaps what was taken was a culture (as in the case of aboriginal people subjected to forcible 're-education' in North America or Australia), or dignity (as in the case of South-East Asian women forced into prostitution by the Japanese army in the Second World War). Redress is still demanded, and sometimes given, or at least attempted. But now, we have moved away from the original simple case in no less than three ways. The person or institution that is called on to redress the wrong is no longer exactly the same person or institution that committed the wrong. The person or institution who is to receive redress is no longer exactly the person or institution who suffered the loss in the first place. And what is to be given, in order to accomplish redress, is no longer exactly the same thing that was wrongly taken – because the thing taken has been destroyed, or dispersed by redistribution, or because what was taken was not a 'thing' in the first place, but something intangible. How can we, in anything like the literal sense of 'give back', *give back* someone's dignity?

So we need to distinguish between three forms that redress might take. 'Restitution' is the clearest: It means that the very thing that was taken is actually returned. Greece wants the Elgin Marbles back (though, understandably, Greek people prefer that the term 'Parthenon Marbles' be used).[10] 'Compensation' is at one remove from that: It means that some equivalent of whatever it was that was taken is given to the person or group that lost it. 'Apology' is an expression of regret that redresses wrongdoing in the weaker but still important sense that it removes any remaining legitimacy from it: It aims to restore the victims' dignity by erasing the view that their loss was justifiable. And as we shall see, all three modes of redress have a place in the issue areas that are especially important for this question today: slavery, colonialism and the dispossession of aboriginal peoples. In all three areas, we see an array of demands and policies, some aimed at the literal return of stolen things, some at compensation for their loss, some at apology – verbal apology, often accompanied by memorial events such as days of recognition, commemorative events or memorial institutions such as museums. Sometimes, demands of all three kinds are combined: At the 2001 World Congress Against Racism, according to *The Guardian* report, African countries made multiple and extensive demands arising from the slave trade and colonialism: 'They include explicit apologies to all victims from individual countries . . . and reparation in the form of debt cancellation, markets open to African exports, health care funding, the return of plundered art objects, and the acceleration of aid.'[11]

All of this, I suggested, comes out of a very simple and common intuition – that wrongs should be righted in ways that somehow benefit their victims. But few if any of the demands and policies aimed at redress are unchallenged. They are often flashpoints of controversy, giving rise to heated political debate. (The demands of African countries at the 2001 Congress, for example, were strongly resisted.) Why, though, if they emerge from so simple a moral idea? The very same – naturally compelling – idea that makes you demand the return of the mountain bike that I stole from your garage last week? The answer, of course, lies in the difference that time makes, or at least seems to make. The flip side of 'you took it, so give it back' is 'but that was then'. When demands for redress are made, some form of the that-was-then response (call it TWTR for short) is almost always what we find among those who object to the demands. Politics does not generally give much time to the distant past; and it is not always a good thing when it does, for societies in which ancient events still weigh heavily are often conflict-ridden and immobilized. (There is such a thing as a 'surfeit of memory'.[12]) So perhaps, it is no surprise that demands for redress are resisted, in the context of a politics that, like ours, is mainly driven by immediate concerns. But if we move to a more reflective level, 'that was then', though crudely put, still captures many of the issues that are raised by demands for historical redress.

'That was then' can, of course, be an impatient or dismissive response to hearing about past injustices – the verbal equivalent of a shrug. That is nothing less than irresponsible. At the very least,

INTRODUCTION

injustices whenever they occur are warnings that should bother us, violations of principles that should mean something to us. Even if, as it eventually turns out, we come to think that no practical response is called for, or is possible, mere indifference is not a response that can be defended from a moral point of view. Being charitable, though, could 'that was then' express a serious point, or perhaps one or more of several serious points? Let us consider what these might be.

Most commonly, I believe, TWTR gets the force it has from the idea that attending to past injustices distracts us from attending to present ones. Our attention is limited, and so are our resources. So if we focus our attention on what, as Canadians, we did to the Louis Riel rebellion (by the *Métis* or mixed-race people) in 1870, or what, as French people, we did to the Protestant minority (the Huguenots) in 1685, or what, as British people, we did to the Irish population of Drogheda in 1649, that may be at the cost of diverting our attention from the injustices that the Canadian, French and British people are currently complicit in. True, there is no reason why French people could not be concerned *both* about the treatment of the Huguenots *and* the circumstances of North African immigrants in the suburbs of Paris today, but political space in France as elsewhere is limited and what the seventeenth-century Huguenots might get, in terms of public attention and exposure, could well be at the expense of what twenty-first-century Moroccans might get. The same goes for resources. If the Canadian government were to give material compensation to the *Métis* people whose political aspirations were brutally crushed in 1870, that might well be at the expense of auto workers in the province of Ontario, who rather frequently experience devastating plant closures that could be prevented or mitigated by financial bail-outs; or of fishing communities experiencing vanishing fish stocks; or of workers in resource industries subject to volatile world demand.

A second justification of TWTR could be this. Much has happened since: True, an injustice occurred long ago, but history has not stood still since then. Many intervening things have taken place. For one thing, those who suffered from the original injustice may subsequently have suffered as a result of events such as wars and recessions, the impact of which was felt by the larger society as well. For another thing, the victims of the original injustice may have made subsequent decisions, bad or unlucky decisions that turned out to affect their subsequent well-being.[13] So it is unreasonable to attribute (the whole of) a group's present condition to a single act of past injustice. True, if the group made bad decisions subsequent to the original injustice, that could be attributed to a degradation of their decision-making capacity that the original injustice brought about: But how far should we go along this road, which could potentially lead to denying the group's agency altogether? At what point do we say, or stop saying, that original victimhood excuses subsequent bad decisions? And finally, while we are thinking about things that might have happened otherwise, how do we know what would have happened to the group in question if it had not been violently dispossessed? Would it have gone on living in just the same way? (How often does *that* happen?) Or would it have adapted to changed circumstances in ways that we can only guess at? Would aboriginal populations have entered a market economy as 'voluntarily' as European populations did? The quotation marks around 'voluntarily' are meant to suggest that voluntariness is always a matter of degree.

A third justification: Standards have changed. 'Back then', all sorts of things were considered justifiable, even worthy, while we find them offensive. In the nineteenth century, for example, museums in North America freely collected the human remains of native peoples, for the purposes of scientific anthropological research. Perhaps (I do not know) they even learned important things by studying native people's skeletons. But we now recognize that, as native societies have made clear, the collection of bones is (at least) as much a desecration for them as the equivalent practice would be for white society. The same goes for the museums' collections of religious artefacts such as masks and pipes, though the collectors' intention in that case was aesthetic rather than scientific. Which standard counts? Are wrongs defined – and, thus, remedies justified or refused – in terms of the

INTRODUCTION

standards of the time, or in terms of our own standards? This issue may not arise as often as is sometimes supposed. More often than not, massive injustices are committed by people who could well know that they were unjust, perhaps knew at some level that they were unjust, but who sheltered themselves by means of the astounding human capacity to make exceptions in arbitrary but convenient ways. History is disturbingly full of examples of this trait, one that may have caused more massive damage than any other. But when the change-of-standards issue does arise in a legitimate way, it confronts the demand for redress with a problem that obliges us not to dismiss the case for TWTR entirely unheard.

A fourth possibility, or perhaps a pair of possibilities (both of which, as we shall see, play a prominent role in the debates on historical redress): The point of TWTR is to tell us that the personnel have changed. At some point or over some period in the past, some group or institution treated some other group unjustly. That is beyond dispute. But if redress is to be made, it means that we have to identify some existing group or institution that we can identify with the original oppressor, and also some existing group that we can identify with the original victim. How is either of those things to be done? Take the identity of the oppressor first. In what sense is anyone or any institution around today identifiable with the persons or institutions that conducted the slave trade, colonized Africa and Asia and forcibly dispossessed aboriginal people? That is not meant to be a rhetorical question at all – perhaps there are continuities: but we have to justify them, as opposed to simply assuming them, if continuity with past actions is to impose responsibilities and costs on anyone, as it should. And take the identity of the victim. Does shared DNA make a person identical to people who suffered terrible losses in the eighteenth century? What if they share DNA with their oppressors? What if, as it happens, they have done rather well since – or if some of them have, so that there is now more inequality within the previously oppressed group than between that group and its previous oppressors? And what if, even if they have not done well, the reasons, as mentioned above, arise from events and decisions that intervened between the eighteenth century and the present? Finally, what are we to make of the worst case of all – one in which subjugation led to the literal disappearance of the victim group (as in the case of the Beothuk people in Newfoundland, a native group that no longer exists) – do we have to find a proxy group to which redress can be made? (And is that still 'redress', if we think of redress as something that victims or descendants get?)

And a final possibility: There were many 'thens', and many things happened, many of them violent and unfortunate, in each 'then'. The possibility of responding accountably to all of them is remote indeed. How are some occurrences picked out as demanding redress, while others are ignored? Here is a cynical view: In some cases, but not others, there are groups that descend from the victims of historical wrongs, groups whose support can be mobilized for political purposes. Some believe that demands for redress arise from the efforts of 'political entrepreneurs', as we may call them, who see an advantage to be won from reminding groups – typically, ethnic groups – of injustices in their past, so that they can be induced to support political objectives. When there is no extant group to be reminded of ancestral wrongs, the wrong is simply forgotten. An example: Among the worst conditions ever suffered by human beings were the conditions endured by the sailors in eighteenth-century European warships. Because mutiny in distant places was dreaded, they were subject to hideous and frequent corporal punishment; in naval battles, because of the tactic of firing broadsides into the beam of ships, they suffered death, blinding and dismemberment by jagged wooden splinters; the medical response was rudimentary and unanaesthetized; and even if there wasn't a battle, their diet, on long voyages, was health destroying.[14] Their lives were probably even worse than the lives of plantation slaves in the American South (and no more voluntarily assumed in many cases, since they too were often 'impressed' or seized). So, why is the horror of slavery commemorated, and redress demanded, while that of eighteenth-century sailors is not? Isn't it all a political matter, as some suggest, disguising itself as a moral one? The descendants of slaves constitute

INTRODUCTION   **13**

an identifiable group, from whose support political capital may be made: The descendants of eighteenth-century sailors don't – so is it really an historical injustice, as such, that worries us, or is that people with survivor claims are still around to cause political bother? (I said this suggestion was cynical – I do not endorse it, and if you feel annoyed, please wait for Chapters 4 and 5, where a quite different explanation is suggested.)

So, to make a case for historical redress, these TWTR objections must be met; it has to be shown, in some way or other, that past events are *not* remote from present responsibilities, despite all the considerations that seem to drive a wedge between what happened long ago and what we should do now. In this, the question that we face is very much like a question that is posed by *global* injustice, or injustices that exist between various countries in the contemporary world. Until recently, those injustices did not get much attention. But in the last few decades, political scientists and philosophers have tried to show that people in wealthy countries are *connected* in some way to people in poorer countries – because they share human rights with them, for example, or because rich countries are part of an economic order that produces poverty in other countries. Just as a good deal has been done to show that there are connections among people who are separated in space, so perhaps it can be shown, too, that there are connections among people separated in time.

How might this be done, though? This book explores the ways in which it might be done. It tries to state the best case for them, and also the objections that they have to overcome. Here is the list of ideas that we will evaluate critically:

1 The rights of the victims of injustice continue beyond their death. We cannot do anything about the harms that they suffered, in the sense of restoring what they lost, because they are not here any more. But the injustice that they suffered was not just a damage to them as persons (a 'harm'), it was an assault on their rights (a 'wrong') – and can we not say that their rights survive them?

2 The benefits of injustice continue to be enjoyed. Perhaps we cannot do anything to restore the loss that was suffered (or even repair the damage to the rights of those who suffered loss). But a benefit was derived from their loss, and injustice continues as long as someone, or some institution, continues to enjoy that benefit. Justice will be done if that benefit is removed.

3 A community (such as a national community) embraces past, present and future. It is in that sense timeless. If we consider ourselves as a community, what happened in the past should continue to be present to us, and how we collectively represent and respond to the past is an essential part of the way in which we define ourselves.

4 Obligations of redress do not arise from the fact that we form a community, they arise from the fact that we are members of a political organization, or state. We may all have very different ideas about what our national community is, or what it owes to anyone. But we are part of a political organization that has responsibilities that extend both backwards and forwards in time. What was done in our name is down to us.

5 Past injustices carry into present inequalities and deprivations. What are called past wrongs are not really *past* wrongs at all. They are important just because they continue into the present. People suffer today because of what was done to their ancestors long ago. And so the reason for caring about past events is simply that we have a reason to worry about and respond to present deprivation and injustice.

These five approaches to the ethics of redress form the basis of the argument of this book. Now you might perhaps find yourself immediately agreeing with some of these views, and being dubious about others. Some, I would agree, look rather more plausible than others do. But as we shall see, they all pose problems that need discussion. For example, (1) asks us to believe that people's rights can in some way survive them, even though it seems natural to think of rights as things

INTRODUCTION 15

that protect people (and perhaps other living beings) against harm: and aren't the deceased entirely beyond harm?; (2) looks as though it will be usable in some cases, especially when some material profit from injustice remains in some person's or group's hands: but not all injustices produce a benefit, surely – who, now, benefits from the Rwandan genocide, for example?; (3) appeals to people who are impressed by the importance of national community to us, and by the importance of the continuity of our ways of life and values. But ways of life and values change, and whether or not we identify ourselves with precursors of, say, the seventeenth century, seems like an open question, to say the least – are there not more similarities between twentieth-century English and Irish people than between English people of the twenty-first and seventeenth centuries?; (4) seems attractive but may be rather undiscriminating, given that most states – especially older states – have done so many things to so many people over time, and have failed to do so many things that they ought to have done, that it may be hard to show that any *particular* deed (or omission) of theirs have any special claim to redress.

Even (5), which is very often taken to be the strongest of all reasons to respond to past injustices, poses problems: for if we place the moral spotlight on present circumstances alone, is it then really (some people ask) *historical* injustice that we are responding to? Or are we just acting on some general view that we hold about what should be done about deprivation and inequality in our society? Let us say we have in mind some level of a decent life, and believe that people who fall below it must be given assistance in reaching it: Does it then matter that we have some historical connection to some group that falls below the line, or would we owe the same, to, say, a group of refugees fleeing oppression elsewhere – oppression in which we played no role at all? Would it matter if the deprivation of some group were to be remedied by, say, a philanthropist (such as George Soros) who had no historical connection with them, as long as something good was done to mitigate severe deprivation? According to some critics of historical redress, that is exactly what we should do: deal with contemporary injustices, wherever they come from, and whoever we are – our history adds nothing significant. So if (5) is to work, we will have to show that history has left particular kinds of damage that give some contemporary wrongs a special claim on us, of a kind that other wrongs do not have.

I do think it can be shown, in ways that Chapter 5 will suggest, that history leaves behind particular kinds of traumatic damage, and that we have to explore the history in order to discover not only their nature but also the remedy for them. Even so, that leaves a further question, for it is not enough to show that remedies are due, we also have to consider the responsibilities of present generations in relation to them. Here the argument is that the clearest way in which current generations come to have responsibility for old wrongs is in reproducing them (as opposed to simply inheriting them). That thought, too, is explored in the same chapter, which puts forward what may look like a rather paradoxical view: that historical redress should matter to us because we should be concerned about transmitting the wrongs of the past to future generations. Whether or not past generations have rights is, as Chapter 1 will suggest, a difficult question that may not get a conclusively positive answer: But future generations *do* much more clearly have rights, and among their rights is a right to clarity about the history that they are born into and benefit or suffer from. They need this if they are to lead just lives. Historical redress, then, is for the sake of the future. Paradoxical, yes, but I think the case for adopting this idea becomes a lot stronger after we have taken a critical look at the alternatives.

As this book goes along, we will discuss many of the examples listed above, and quite a few others. And in the Conclusion, we will try to assess what has been shown. Does it help us towards resolving any of these issues? Please bear in mind, though, that the main point of this book is not to persuade you that any of these issues should be resolved in one way or another, but, rather, to explore in a critical way the *kinds of arguments* that are used to support or deny redress.

1
DOES THE PAST HAVE RIGHTS?

Many atrocious things have happened in the past. Anyone with any sort of moral sense, however primitive, must regret them deeply, and not to regret them is to read oneself out of the human race. 'Regret' is of course far too tame a word – many appalling things in the past horrify, disgust and distress us, and may literally go beyond our comprehension. But we can regret and even be horrified and disgusted by things without always having a responsibility to do anything about them. Some, for example, may be distanced from us by space – if we are not Japanese, our responsibility (as distinct from our revulsion) is not engaged by the atrocities committed by the Japanese army in Nanking, China, in 1937: not at all because we do not think they were horrific – we have seen the newsreel footage – but because they are not *ours*. Others may be very distant in time – the pitiless ways in which the Roman Empire punished slave rebellions, for example, or in which medieval European societies treated witches or heretics. So if we have to make redress for any past injustices, those injustices must be shown to survive, in some way or other, in our present. They have to be somehow connected to us. As the Introduction suggested, this may be the most difficult single issue posed by the idea of historical redress, from an ethical point of view.

Perhaps the hardest case of all to deal with is the sort that involves deceased generations. When survivors of past atrocity or oppression still live, we can do something – however inadequate – for them. There are survivors of British oppression in Kenya (who are actively pressing their case for redress, at the time of writing): Some South-East Asian 'comfort women' still live, and demand apology and reparations from Japan; there are survivors of the residential schools that were forcibly imposed on native populations in North America and Australia; there is a dwindling number of Holocaust survivors. It is not too much of a stretch to add the victims' immediate relatives, whose lives were transformed by their loss, to this list. Alternatively, when some object – land, an artefact – was wrongfully taken, it may still exist even if its original owners do not, and we can at least think about what ought to be done with it: Should looted art, for example, be restored to its country of origin? But when a wrong was done to people's lives or freedom or dignity, and those who suffered it are now deceased, an especially severe version of the 'that was then' issue, mentioned above, comes into play: not only was *that* then, some might say, *they* were then, and the idea of making redress seems at least one large step removed from what we might do in terms of compensating living survivors or victims' close relatives, or returning some existing object to its historical owner. It is not the distance in time, as such, that explains why no claims for redress arise from the Crusades, but, as one writer has said, 'the lack of claimants'.[1]

For that reason, it is attractive to think about the idea that although victims of wrongdoing do not themselves survive, something about them, some important feature or property of theirs, does survive; and the most promising avenue is to consider whether or not their *rights* do. If so, that opens up the possibility that although we can do nothing for them as persons, we can still think about ways of doing something about their rights, as things that in some way represent them or stand in for them in the present. That makes some idea of redress at least thinkable, and if a case can be made out, it will lead us to a distinctive (and important) position. For as we shall see in later chapters, approaches to redress frequently stake out their position in relation to present circumstances: the present effects of past injustice, for example, or the present possession of what was once unjustly taken away. Uniquely, however, the approach based on the 'rights of the past' addresses itself to something that can be done for those who are deceased – that is, to respect their rights. This may seem, initially at least, a puzzling idea; but, if nothing else, it has the great merit of focusing on past injustice itself, rather than on its present effects. So, convincing or not, it is certainly on point.

This chapter discusses three versions of the 'surviving rights' approach. The first version draws on the familiar idea that we respect the rights of deceased people when we execute their wills and fulfil promises made to them: Does this show that past generations can have rights, in a way that could make sense of historical redress? The second concerns victims of injustice who have surviving descendants: Can we say that the victims had an interest in the well-being of their descendants, and so, perhaps, a right that we should treat them well? The third concerns people who were killed, or whose lives were drastically shortened, by oppressive regimes, and it draws upon a paradox that has intrigued philosophers: If we are to say (as surely we do) that their rights were violated, doesn't that mean that we *must* believe in posthumous rights – in rights that continue after the death of those who possessed them?

The chapter will argue that the first and second of these approaches do not do what we need to do in order to arrive at a theory of redress. The third comes closer, although it may initially look like a bit of detour, and also has to take a twist and turn in order to become usable for our purposes in this book. But before all this gets under way, we need to pause for a moment to think about the idea of rights itself: Why are people's rights so important that their survival into the present – even if it could be demonstrated – would make a difference to what we should do?

Why rights matter

Rights are very powerful things, from an ethical point of view. They cannot properly be ignored, or set aside just because it is convenient for governments or societies to do so, even if by doing so they could do things that would otherwise be considered good. Rights, according to one very influential statement, are 'trumps over some background justification for political decisions that states a goal for the community as a whole'.[2] In this way, rights differ from ordinary 'interests'. We can of course hope (if we are optimists) that all our interests will be protected, and do what we can to see that they will be, but we cannot say that we are actually entitled to their protection, or that we are wronged if someone overrides them. I have an interest, for example, in being allowed to park my car outside my house as long as I wish, that is to say, I can derive some advantages from being allowed to do so, in terms of pursuing various purposes of importance to me. But suppose traffic on my street greatly increases and the city decides that to maintain good traffic flow, the street must have four clear lanes with no parking allowed: My interest may (and reasonably) be overridden by the interests of the larger number of people who need my street to become a free-flowing traffic artery. Rights, however, cannot be overridden just like that. I have a right to a fair trial, for example, and the government must not dispense with a fair trial just because the courts are really busy right now, or because it wants to make an example of my misdeeds in a prompt and efficient way. It has to bear the costs of providing people with trials, costs that are very considerable, for they include not only the direct costs of maintaining courts, prosecutors and defence lawyers, but also a whole infrastructure of legal education so that such things as courts and lawyers can exist, plus a whole system of policing and detection and punishment so that trials can be conducted and their outcomes enforced.[3] If rights were overridden by a refusal to pay the cost of protecting them, they would mean nothing at all.

That is not to say that rights cannot ever be overridden. One right, after all, may have to be overridden, or at least compromised in some way, because it conflicts with some other right. (That is the limitation of the 'trump' metaphor quoted above – sometimes, as is not the case in the game of bridge, it is as though there is more than one trump.[4]) My indisputable right to play my favourite Cajun music may have to be constrained, at night, in consideration of my neighbour's equally indisputable right to sleep. My indisputable right to my property may have to be overridden if you need to cross my land in an emergency – if the straightest route to the hospital happens to be across my front lawn. But rights are at least very hard to override or compromise: They demand our serious attention, and only something very compelling, such as a still more urgent right, can override what they require.

So, if it is true that the victims of past injustices have rights that survive their death, the injustices that they suffered will demand attention even if it would be convenient to ignore them, or annoyingly expensive to respect them. (Trials, as just noted, are very expensive – but we still have a right to them.) People alive now would not be free to ignore them: They would amount to strong constraints on policies that governments, or voters, might really much prefer to adopt or pay for, if they could get away with it. Rights, in short, are ethically important obstacles to things that might be convenient to do – such as, notably, forgetting the past. And attending to them is not an optional matter, or one that falls into the realm of our discretion, or our freedom to follow our preferences or do things to suit our own interests. Can we say, though, that the rights of past generations have this sort of compelling force? If so, the case for redress will be very attractive.

The testamentary model

When the topic of the rights of deceased people comes up, it is both common and natural to think of what looks like a really simple case: the right of people that their legal wills should be executed. This is certainly a familiar case in which it makes sense to think of deceased people as having rights that survive their death. But – unfortunately for this version of the argument for historical redress – it does not do what is needed to support that argument. While they are alive, people (or most people) have a strong interest in what happens to things that they have worked for, or else value for some other reason, after their death. Legal arrangements for the making and execution of wills reflect and respect this interest, which is actually best thought of as an interest of *living* people, even though it bears upon what happens after their death. To be sure, we continue to respect and execute wills after the death of those who have made them, but unless we had this ongoing practice, the whole business of making wills would, obviously, make no sense at all, and the interest of living people in distributing their property would not be respected. So what is really at stake is the interest of living people, not of deceased people, in the reliability of a social and legal arrangement.[5]

A generation of cynical and unfeeling people could refuse to honour wills on the grounds that those who had made them could no longer know or care about whether or not they were honoured. But then the cynical and unfeeling generation would not be entitled to rely on the practice themselves, knowing that their descendants would be entitled to be no less cynical and unfeeling than they were. (The idea that each generation has obligations to the past as part of a 'chain' of this kind is an important idea that we shall discuss in Chapter 4.) When we say, then, that deceased people have a right that their wills be honoured and executed, we are really talking about rights that make sense as part of an accepted, established intergenerational practice that, just because it is an ongoing one, creates expectations that certain things will be done. There clearly isn't any such thing, though, in the case of the sort of events that attract historical redress. There isn't an established legal practice here that gives people rights. Rather, the argument is reversed in this case, the idea of rights preceding the practice, and calling for it, instead of following from it: because oppressed people had rights, the argument goes, we must develop a new practice that respects them. For the practice of respecting the rights of people certainly is not one that victims of chronic oppression could, when living, have relied upon – what they were painfully accustomed to, in fact, was a system that was based on the wholesale and systematic violation of their rights. So we have to explain its basis in some other and quite different way – not in terms of their 'expectations'.

DOES THE PAST HAVE RIGHTS?

The second case that naturally comes to mind, that of making promises to people on their deathbed, leads to the same sort of result. If a dying person asks you to look after, say, his or her library of precious books, and you promise to do so, we do not suppose that, as soon as he or she dies, you are free to pack up the book collection and take it to Sotheby's for auction, on the grounds that the person in question would not know about it. But again, it seems that the best way to explain this is in terms of the interest of living people in maintaining a practice – not a legal one this time, but an ethical one. We think the practice of making promises is important to the way human life is carried on, we know it could not be carried on if people were free to break promises when, for any reason, they could do so without consequences for themselves, and so deathbed promises should be honoured for much the same reason as wills.[6] So again, what we need for historical redress is some kind of argument that does not depend (only) on the interest of living people in maintaining some kind of practice. What we need is an argument that shows that rights survive death even when their survival does not depend on some important interest of people who are still alive. Otherwise, isn't it much simpler and more compelling to explain what is required in terms of the unproblematic idea that living people have important interests?

We (meaning here people in Western societies) do not always act as though we had obligations to respect what deceased people expressly wanted, and in some cases, it isn't even entirely clear that we should.[7] A case in point is the archaeological exploration of buried remains.[8] When kings in ancient times caused themselves to be buried, with their prized possessions, in elaborately defended structures, they could hardly have made it plainer that they wished their remains to be undisturbed. But exploration of their tombs is so crucial an activity in understanding ancient civilizations that their wishes are hardly likely to be respected. (Ironically, of course, it is exactly the monumental nature of the defences that they built that attracts the attention of both altruistic archaeologists and mercenary tomb robbers.) Shakespeare's gravestone, in Stratford-Upon-Avon, is inscribed with a simple rhymed plea that his remains not be disturbed: but it is very doubtful indeed that this plea would be honoured if DNA analysis were to be needed in order to settle disputes about the identity of a national cultural icon. No doubt our willingness to disturb graves reflects the fact that we give no credence to the ideas that led the deceased to forbid the practice: We do not accept pre-Christian beliefs that deceased kings would need their ships and jewellery in the afterlife, or – most of us – Christian beliefs in the resurrection of the body. But, actually, that only makes the point more strongly. Not only are we prepared to violate what particular deceased people would have demanded as something due to them, we are also prepared, it seems, to discount whole schemes of belief within which their demands made sense to them.

Our interests survive us

But let us turn to the second model. The case of African slavery is best suited to bring it into play. While the slave trade was in operation, about 14 million Africans were seized and transported, under vile conditions, to plantations and households in North and South America and the Caribbean. (There are several estimates of the numbers: Some are higher, some lower.) Legally classified as property rather than as people, their most basic interests as human beings were systematically violated. They were physically abused, sometimes branded or otherwise mutilated. They were compelled to work under harsh and degrading conditions. They were subjected without recourse to the arbitrary will of their owners. They could be bought and sold. No one who knows anything of the facts of African slavery could refuse to believe that a response to them is called for, even though so much time has passed – doubts, if any, arise only because no response seems anywhere near adequate, because the damage that was suffered is beyond repair.

But is it? Perhaps one of the victims' major interests survives. No one could doubt that the disruption of families, and the terrible

DOES THE PAST HAVE RIGHTS?

prospects that slaves knew to face their children, were among the most unbearable costs of slavery. Slaves were drawn from a cultural background in which family life was highly valued; and in the conditions in which they were compelled to live, family life was – if they were lucky – the only area in which they could enjoy any of the essential features of a human life. And we can certainly suppose that, among their interests, there was an interest in promoting the well-being of their descendants. One philosopher has written:

> One of the ways in which we can benefit the dead, if we can benefit them at all, is by promoting the welfare of their descendants. Most slaves probably cared very much about the welfare of their descendants, so the United States could provide *reparations to the slaves* by promoting the welfare of their descendants.[9]

I have put part of this quote in italics in order to stress the point that, in this argument – as distinct from the arguments that we will consider in Chapters 2 and 5 – it is the deceased slaves themselves, not living African-Americans, who are owed something. While we can no longer do anything, for example, to remedy the inhumanly cruel and often lethal conditions that were suffered by slaves as they crossed the Atlantic, promoting their descendants' well-being is actually within our grasp. Their descendants exist, and there are certainly things that can be done to promote their well-being: affirmative action policies in employment, admissions quotas in professional schools, scholarship programmes and so on. Even acts of redress of a non-material kind, such as memorial events recognizing the wrong of slavery, could be understood as contributions to the slaves' descendants' well-being, to the extent that, in some more indirect way, they tend to improve their relative social position by diminishing prejudices against them.

I see no reason why, if we decide that this interest of deceased slaves survives, we should not speak of it in terms of *rights*. It meets all the standard tests. Above, to be sure, we distinguished rights from *ordinary* interests, or interests that can simply be overridden when it is convenient to do so, but rights can be seen as protecting interests of a particular kind, that is, interests that have a special importance to human life, an importance that my interest in parking outside my house does not have. Like, for example, physical security, they have to have an importance that affects many areas of my life – a 'strategic' importance, we might say, in that whether or not I have them exercises a pervasive effect over the kind of life I can have, not just over my ability to do this or that particular thing. Without security, to take the clearest example, there aren't that many particular things we can do, unless we happen to be very lucky, always, in our circumstances. To qualify for the protection of rights, the interests would also have to have *general* importance, that is, they cannot be based on some idiosyncratic interest of mine but must be based on the idea of an opportunity or a resource that all or most lives can be said to depend on. Personal security and subsistence, for example – unlike even an intense desire for an Armani suit or a new cell phone – pass this demanding test, and so it is generally supposed that rights should protect them. They are things that people need whatever their personal or idiosyncratic goals in life. And I do not think there can be much doubt that people's interests in the welfare of their children have an equally 'strategic' or central place in their lives. If so, then the case that we are considering looks very plausible: Violations of the rights of the deceased are *not*, in one limited but very important respect, beyond repair, and, as we have just seen, some perfectly workable policies are available for repairing them. So perhaps here we have a surviving right of the deceased, one that has important consequences for social policy and law.

All this, however, runs into a snag at once: Valuable though rights are, we would not be able to attribute them to deceased people if it were true, as some claim, that only existing people can have rights. For something to have anything at all, one view is, it has to exist in the first place.[10] If you have a car, for example, then it makes sense to say that it has four doors or two: If you do not have a car, it makes no sense to say that it 'has' any number of doors. That seems to me to rest far too much on a claim about how language is used, and it is not even clear that it is true. Surely, even imaginary beings can be said to 'have' attributes? Within the context of Charles Dickens's novel, *Martin Chuzzlewit*, Mrs Gamp, although a fictional creation, 'has' an umbrella that is an important part of her character. And wished-for things can have attributes too – 'If I had a house', I might say, longingly, 'it would have a garden just like that one'. If imaginary and wished-for items can be said to have things, it seems unlikely that deceased people – who at least *once* had real existence – should be seen as more incapable of having things than entities that have never existed at all.

A rather better argument is that rights are significant things because they enable people to exercise choice and to get other people to respect them – something that non-existent people obviously cannot do. This is an argument that makes a lot of sense if we focus on certain kinds of rights, such as property rights. You have a property right in your house or apartment. That means you can make decisions about how to decorate and furnish it and about who to admit into it to admire your decoration and furnishing, and if anyone tries to obstruct your choices in either of those respects, you will have an enforceable claim to prevent them. If design guru Martha Stewart objected to your proposed colour palette, or if socialite Paris Hilton wanted to use your space for some festive purpose, you could stop them, because that is what it means to have a right to your property. That is all quite true, but it does not cover everything about what it means to have rights, and it seems wrong to model rights in general on considerations that apply only to some particular kinds of rights, such as property rights.[11]

For some kinds of rights can be exercised on behalf of whoever it is that they belong to. Welfare agencies claim rights on behalf of young children. People claim rights on behalf of relatives who are in a coma in hospital. Recent legislation in Switzerland establishes legal officers charged with protecting the rights of animals (including the rights of goldfish and canaries to be provided with companions, in recognition of their status as social animals). So the fact that non-existent people cannot make claims on their own behalf does not mean they cannot have rights. If we accept that view, then we can make sense of the rights of the non-existent by supposing that rights protect interests that are real and important even if no one currently possesses or claims them. Proxies can claim them on behalf of those who cannot make claims, and we could adopt that solution in the case of deceased people as we do in many others.

But should we speak of 'interests', and of the kinds of interests that ought to be protected as 'rights', only in cases in which some living being stands to gain or lose something, now or in the future? In which, in other words, some gain or loss will actually be experienced? Or will lead to some feeling, of a positive or negative kind? Of course, if we were to adopt policies (such as affirmative employment policies) for the descendants of African slaves, that would lead to an experienced gain on *their* part, but that, as we have just seen, is not what the argument needs: *This* argument is not based on the interests or rights of the descendants of slaves, but on the interests and rights of their ancestors. And so, if the possession of interests and rights depends on the capacity to *experience* gains and losses, the argument fails at once, and advocates of redress will have to find another way to support their case.

In one of the ways in which we talk about 'interests', it is certainly true that having an interest is a matter of having an experience of some kind. Sometimes, when we speak of people's interests, we mean things that interest them, or things that they take an interest in. In this sense, people's interests include such things as salsa dancing, trainspotting, philosophy, Indonesian cuisine – meaning that these are activities that engage people's attention and curiosity, absorb their time and energy and bring their conversation to life. Now it is pretty clear that only living persons can be 'interested' in this sense, for only those who currently live have such things as attention and curiosity to devote to something, or conversation to enliven. And the interest of living persons in something can exist only for as long as it is engaged – someone's interest in Indonesian cuisine evaporates at the very moment at which it begins to bore them. But there is a second way of talking about interests that is not limited in this way. For

DOES THE PAST HAVE RIGHTS?

something can be 'in (or else against) someone's interest' without him or her being aware of it at all. Suppose some long-lost (wealthy) aunt has named me as a beneficiary in her will, without my knowledge? Much less pleasantly, it is possible that, as I write this, some distant enemy, to whom I have unwittingly given offence, is blackening my name by spreading the news that I am guilty of armed piracy, or of parking in handicapped spots: That is certainly against my interest, even if I never find out about it. Can we say, though, as some theorists do, that unknown slanders of that kind are against my interest only because they could potentially become known (and thus painful) to me, or else because third parties who hear about them might change their behaviour towards me, in ways that damage my interests (even if I never discover the reason why)?[12] This is disputed; but perhaps we can say that unperceived dangers are against one's interest because they are the *sort of thing* that would be damaging if they came to light. It is not exactly the potential of their coming to light that makes them damaging, rather it is the character that they would have if they did come to light. A quietly muttered threat, for example, amounts to a threat because it would be a threat if it were heard, not because or to the extent that there is some chance that it may be heard. And surely it is right that we would want to call such a thing a 'threat' even before it became known to the threatened person, or even if it never did.

We could call the interests that depend on someone's taking an interest 'subjective interests' and the interests that can be promoted or damaged without the subject's knowledge 'objective interests'. Can we say that while non-existent people cannot have subjective interests (because they are not aware of anything), they can have objective interests (the sort that does not depend on having awareness)? If so – returning to our case – there is no obstacle to saying that an important interest of deceased slaves survives, and that its violation can and must be remedied, even if doing so limits the freedom of some presently existing people and diminishes the resources available to them. If people don't have to know what is happening to their interests, then they don't have to be alive in order to have them. Their interests can be posthumously promoted: Deceased slaves' interest in their descendants can be promoted, and so too – extending the argument – can deceased aboriginal people's interest in the survival of their culture, since it is in the power of present generations to affect what happens to it.

Can the dead be harmed?

Now some people take the view that this way of thinking involves the bizarre idea that time can run backwards. Saying that someone can be affected by things that happen after their death is like saying that a later event can affect an earlier one. If someone died on 3 August 1999, it does not seem that their life can be affected by something terrible that happened on 4 August 1999, without supposing that we have to suspend the common-sense rule that while earlier events can affect later ones, later events cannot affect earlier ones. It is a bit like saying that someone was unwell in the morning because his or her dinner was going to give him or her food poisoning later in the day. While that is obviously wrong, perhaps we should balance the argument by another consideration. Although later events cannot *cause* earlier ones, what something *is* can be affected by what happens at a later point in time. For example, a historian can properly say that 'the Seven Years War broke out in 1756', even though it was not until 1763, when it ended, that it became possible to call it 'the Seven Years War'. Likewise, the way in which we describe someone's life may depend on later considerations. If later considerations, based on things that happen after their death, change the way in which we characterize their life, doesn't that change their life? Won't we see the lives of the oppressed differently if the story of their people ends up one way rather than another – well rather than badly?

Let us fancifully imagine that some time ago there was a Shakespearean scholar who devoted his life to proving that Shakespeare was a woman. Items of information in the plays, turns

DOES THE PAST HAVE RIGHTS?

of phrase employed in them, the kind of moral sensibility displayed by them – all this, he claimed, proved that the plays had a female author. He died, though, without amassing any more circumstantial proof than dozens of others had gathered in favour of their own pet theories, and so was written off as just one of many crackpot critics in Shakespearean studies. But then, a few years after his death, a proof of his theory appeared – a letter, in Shakespeare's own hand, that said: 'My name is Wilma. I call myself "Will" because a girl can't get work in this business' (or words to that effect). Our critic suddenly becomes a cultural hero. But then, things change again, because it is alleged that the letter in question was a clever forgery by the Warwickshire Women's Collective, a group committed to recovering and celebrating the role of women in literary history. So our critic becomes a loser again. But then, a bit later, it turns out that the allegations of forgery were made by a suspect organization with a history of devious anti-feminist propaganda . . . and the story goes on.[13] The later, then cannot actually cause changes in the earlier, but, it seems, it can significantly change its character, or how it is properly described. What is true about its character can change if knowledge changes. And what we take to be knowledge certainly does change.

So interests survive, and lives can be changed after the fact, as it were. But from an ethical point of view, surely we care about whether people's interests get to be hindered or promoted only because they are *harmed* if their interests are hindered or not promoted. Certainly if one wishes, one can detach interests from people and talk about them as being hindered or promoted, even if the people are not there. That is not an absurd thing to do, given the way language works. But damage to people's interests matters because it harms the people who have the interests, and if the people in question are beyond harm – because they no longer exist – then although it is perfectly possible or meaningful to go on talking about damage to their interests, it no longer matters. Likewise, we can certainly talk about 'lives' being changed by posthumous events, detaching 'lives' – rather as we may detach 'interests' – from the people who own them, and thus from the experience of the people who own them: but again, we may object that the moral point has been lost – that how a life is described is important to the person in question only if they might be affected by how it is described.[14]

We could put both of these objections under a single heading, that of 'harm'. Only the living can be harmed; and if, as seems plausible, we think of rights as things that can protect people against harm, and as being important for that reason, then the deceased should not be said to have rights. We can complicate the picture as much as we like by detaching interests from the people who have them, and the character of lives from those who live them, but the bedrock fact remains that the reason for valuing rights at all depends on the existence, in the land of the living, of those whose rights they are, because they are vulnerable to the loss of those important interests that rights are meant to protect. So, may we conclude that the dead, although they can be said to have interests, cannot be harmed, and so have no rights?

Posthumous rights and cold cases

No, or not yet anyway, for we need to shift to something far more brutal. Many slaves were killed. Many aboriginal people were killed in the course of dispossessing them of land. Many victims of Spanish, British, Dutch, Portuguese, French, German and Belgian colonialism were killed. Many prisoners of war in Japanese prison camps were killed. Many Japanese people were killed by the atomic bombs dropped on Hiroshima and Nagasaki. Pick any or all of those examples that you regard as wrongful killing. That topic brings us to the last line of defence for the idea of posthumous rights. This is the claim that, unless people have posthumous rights, it cannot be a rights-violation to kill them. Since if anything at all is a rights-violation, then surely wrongful killing is, and that is a reason to take this view seriously.

How does the view work? It is very simple, though paradoxical looking. If you are wrongfully killed, you are wrongfully killed at the moment of your death, not a moment before – while you are still alive, obviously you have not been wrongfully killed. So if only living people can have rights, rights are not violated by murder: for the right is violated only at the moment of their death, and if dead people do not have rights, there is no longer a right there to be violated, at that point. If we think, then, as surely we do, that murder is a rights-violation, it must be that deceased people do have rights after all. Of course, the person in question, while living, may have suffered the fear of death – but suppose they were humanely and instantly dispatched by death-rays? And of course, other people may become worried by the murder, but that does not explain why it is the victim's own rights, rather than the rights of worried neighbours, that are violated. So if we want to explain why the murdered person's own rights have been violated, it seems that we have to say that the dead *do* have rights. And that opens the door, once again, to supposing that the rights of the millions of people whose deaths have been caused or hastened by oppression are with us still, demanding a response.

The view we are considering – that unless deceased people have rights there would be no right against murder – would be defeated if there were a point between life and death, a point at which death-is-succeeding-life – the 'moment of loss', we could call it. At that moment, it could be said of the person that he or she was alive (and so had rights) and also that he or she had been murdered (the process of dying was under way). This is by no means absurd: In the field of medical ethics, after all, it is in fact very far from clear that there is a decisive single point of transition from life to death. (True, our legal systems require us to certify an exact 'time of death', but how that point is defined may not match up with what medicine, or ethics, or philosophy, or common sense, may say. It is based on nothing more than legal convention.) That line of thought may appeal to readers of an ancient Greek philosopher, Zeno, who proposed that, however minutely we try to divide up time, we can always divide it more minutely still. Between the living person and the murdered person, there would be an in-between person in the process of undergoing loss. But Zeno's own argument provides a reply. However close you suppose one point to be to the next, we can always sneak another one in, and so one could subdivide the 'moment of loss' into two even finer points that would make life and death distinct again. Of course, the posthumous-rights sceptic could then insert another point between those two so as to reinsert an intermediate state . . . but as you will see, this is a game that no one could hope to win, because the process could go on for ever.

But a summary discussion such as this is necessarily going to produce indeterminate results of that sort, because what is at issue here brings into play two of the oldest and most disputed problems in the history of philosophy, which we can hardly expect to be rapidly resolved. One is the ancient topic of the 'badness of death', a topic famously introduced by another ancient Greek philosopher, Epicurus, who held that the deprivation of life could not be a misfortune because, by definition, no one living experienced the deprivation. Is the almost universal fear of death entirely irrational, therefore? Another is the topic of personal identity: Is a person a 'mind-plus-body' so that when either the mind or the body dies, the person dies too? Perhaps, rather, a person is an appearance in the social world, an appearance that does not instantly fade with his or her physical death?[15] It is not possible to do more than mention, let alone settle, even a few of these issues here.[16]

To step around this nest of intractable problems, let us try a different line of thinking altogether. In television dramas and to some extent (surely it must be a lesser extent!) in real life, police forces and public prosecutors investigate 'cold cases', cases, that is, in which any hope of a conviction was at some point abandoned, but which for some reason attract attention again. They are almost always murder cases, so by definition, the victims are deceased, and in some cases, the perpetrators too may be deceased, or at any rate cannot be known to be living at the point at which the investigation begins. So, although much smaller in scale, they are somewhat like the 'ancient wrongs' that lead to demands for historical redress. The fact that they are investigated shows that *something* of the past event survives into the present, and the fact that the premise sustains a good deal of television drama shows that there must be a widespread sense of justice that makes people feel that injustice does not fade away simply because time passes. And I think that may give us an important clue. We have seen some reasons to doubt that people's rights survive them. But perhaps we should say, instead, that violations of their rights survive them? That there is still a *case* to be answered, even though it is a cold one?

Now you may perhaps feel, quite understandably, that this is a simple impossibility, for unless something exists, it cannot be violated. If my bank account is empty, you cannot steal from it. If I do not have a house you cannot burgle it. So if I do not have rights, how can you violate them? But if I once had money in my bank account, it is possible that you once stole from it, and if I once had a house, it is possible that you burgled it. If you did, nothing that subsequently happens – closing the bank account, selling the house – will expunge those events from the record of what previously occurred. They are still brute facts, and significant ones. So is there perhaps a sense in which violations last longer than the rights that were violated? A sense in which violations stay on the moral record even if we are not sure whether the victims, when deceased, can be thought of as bearing rights?

This may look a bit strange, but there is really not much of a mystery about it, although to clear it up, we have to shift the focus of discussion slightly but significantly. People, we may perhaps decide, do stop having rights when they cease to exist. Violations of rights go on existing, however – they stay on the record – because rights continue to exist. But the rights that go on existing are not rights that we should think of as features or properties of particular, determinate people: they are not belongings of this or that person – like his or her estate, or reputation – but rights that are features or properties of anyone, living or dead. Murder is a violation of a right to personal security, theft is a violation of a property right. Particular violations do not fade away, because the ideas that underlie the rights are important ones – important not just to those who suffered violations, but to all those to whom they are important.

There is a good way to confirm the truth of this: Consider other cases in which things that may once have been called 'rights' have, thanks to a change in moral standards, become incredible. We do not, for example, uphold the claims of slave owners to the compensation that they thought they were entitled to when they were dispossessed of slaves. We do not uphold the claims of husbands to privileges that they lost when marital rape was criminalized. Violations of rights remain on the account, as it were, only when or to the extent that the rights in question retain what we could call their moral currency with us. While a right's moral currency remains good, we do not have to justify protecting it, or remedying its violation, on the grounds that it is still a right of some particular person or group. (Remembering that it was once theirs, and how they came to be deprived of it, is of course still an essential part of recording and insisting upon its importance; but its importance does not spring from the fact that it was uniquely *theirs*, like a personal possession, but, rather, from the fact that they shared it with others.)

The 'too abstract' objection

But is there a risk here, as some believe, that of substituting something general and abstract for something particular and concrete?[17] It is as though we were saying that what matters about slavery is that some basic security rights were violated, not that some 14 million people suffered some very particular and atrocious hardships as a result of a long-sustained practice. Not only that, but the very particular atrocities that slaves endured are much more moving, when we see representations of them, than any abstract and general statement about the rights that people have. Novels and movies about the slave experience are very much more compelling than the dry experience of reading the *Universal Declaration of Human Rights*. That is surely true. A simple, chilling, diagram of a slave ship does more to drive home the point than reading the work of great moral philosophers can do. The hundreds of thousands who were slaughtered in the First World War are represented, we may note, by the Tomb of *the* Unknown Soldier – not by a (descriptively very much more appropriate) mass grave. Charities such as Oxfam and World Vision have learned that donations are more strongly motivated by particular representations of deprivation than by general accounts of deprivation. And many psychological studies suggest that moral sensitivity is strangely numbed, not (as we might suppose) enhanced, by the scale of suffering. But these considerations seem to cut both ways. If the suffering of one particular child is more compelling than the suffering of the human race as a whole, then the suffering of one particular child is also more compelling than the suffering of 14 million people. We cannot imaginatively grasp the suffering of 14 million people any more easily than we can grasp the suffering of all humanity – once we pass a certain threshold of scale, everything becomes 'abstract', and if we memorialize only the fully concrete and individual, we will rule much of history out of memory: including slavery and genocide, or anything else that millions have suffered.

We do seem to have a primitive moral capacity, though, to generalize from particular cases to general ones. It is true that charitable donors may respond more readily to a picture of one distressed African child than to statistics about the scale of distress in African countries. But it is quite unnecessary to suppose that the donors who respond believe that particular African child to be the only African child in need. They see her, surely, as a typical case whose particular attributes bring home to them an immense problem, and they would not respond to her condition so strongly unless they thought so – unless they saw the child as disturbingly emblematic as well as touchingly individual. We can much more easily see general need in a particular case than when the general need is abstractly presented, but we should not take that as meaning that people simply do not care about general needs at all – it just means that sometimes they have to be hooked in by particular representations of them. So, following up this line of thought, I do not see why the conclusion suggested above expresses any sort of disregard for or insensitivity to the case at hand. Saying that slaves suffered wrongs that would be atrocious to impose on any human does not diminish the fact that it was certain humans, and not others, who suffered them. We do not disrespect their particularity by taking their suffering as an example of a wrong whose severity is of universal and enduring importance. And in fact, taking the point one step further, if we did not think that what they suffered would be experienced as suffering by any human who was subjected to it, would we even be able to think of it as suffering at all? Sure, all suffering is specific suffering. But if it was *entirely* specific (and so unrelated to anyone else's experience) we could not even grasp why it amounts to suffering. As Bernhard Schlink (author of *The Reader*, a novel and later a movie) has written, in connection with the Holocaust, the appeal to uniqueness is double-edged: It elevates, but also neutralizes. People who insisted on the uniqueness of the Holocaust, wishing it to be a warning to future generations, 'defeated their own purpose. Future generations can be warned by the Holocaust not to do something they are about to do only if what they are about to do is somehow comparable to the Holocaust'.[18]

If that is our solution, however, we need to look elsewhere for the basic reason for the need for redress. If redress is called for because of belief in the enduring importance of a set of rights, rather than in the persistence, into our present, of the rights specifically belonging to the deceased, we still need to know why that set of rights requires that past violations of it still matter. We cannot just assert that, because the rights are important, past violations matter too – that *is* much too abstract a claim. Rights matter because of their practical consequences. They are not just theoretical constructs, they relate to features of human life that demand active and engaged attention and respect, features that are connected with our shared vulnerabilities to loss and danger. We value them because they play a crucial role in reducing our vulnerability. Obviously, when people's vulnerabilities have been denied or exploited in the past, it is now too late to do anything to reduce them: So why, if the belief in rights is *practically* motivated – that is, motivated by a desire to make a difference to the world – should we still insist on the importance of past violations that are now beyond our practical reach? Are past violations useful to us just as reminders of an often vivid kind – so that they would be replaceable, in principle, by skillfully crafted fictional ones? (Would *Huckleberry Finn*, or *To Kill a Mocking-Bird*, do instead?) That thought certainly does seem to reduce their standing drastically. But why would we want past violations to enjoy more respect than that?

As the following chapters try to show, there are several possible ways of answering that question. Here is one view that comes into play at once, given the issues discussed in this chapter: We need to recall past violations because some, in the present, still benefit from them. It is unconscionable that violations of rights should be forgotten, and should attract no response, to the extent that some continue to benefit from their violation – that, on this view, is why we take a practical interest. Those who benefit may be among us. Or perhaps we ourselves are the ones who benefit. In either case, it is often said that a responsibility falls to us for that reason, a reason that the next chapter examines.

2
WHO BENEFITS?

This chapter examines an approach that is quite different from the survival-of-rights approach discussed in the previous chapter – in fact, we may see it as exactly the other side of the coin. We can think of the *loss* as continuing, in the form of a violated right; or we can think, rather, of the *benefit* that arose from the loss as continuing, in someone's hands, as we speak. To return to the case of the stolen mountain bike: It is not that your loss somehow endures forever (or, if, as they say, 'nothing lasts forever', at least indefinitely) but that I continue to benefit from it as long as I still have the bike, or whatever it is that I sold or traded it for. The continued enjoyment of the benefit is what makes the original wrong endure, as well as giving rise to a liability for doing something about it. So, on this view: It is not that you lost something, it is that we gained it – and have it still, right now. Who has benefited, then, on this view, is the key question.

A benefit is certainly more tangible and demonstrable than a violated right. Critics of rights often complain that rights are abstractions or fictions, airy and imaginary things that we cannot point to or touch – like unicorns, one (especially severe) critic says;[1] so a violation of a right, from their point of view, would be abstract twice over, a negation of a fiction and thus completely odd and mysterious – rather like complaining about the scarcity of unicorns, perhaps. Benefits are more appealingly concrete, however. You can actually discover the stolen mountain bike in my garage (or the dubiously acquired marble sculptures that draw visitors to my museum). More significantly, you can point to the accumulated profits of slavery and colonialism in the hands of certain people or institutions or societies, even though slavery and colonialism (in their original forms) are no longer practised.

That is one advantage. Another is that those who retain the profits evidently have in their hands the means of compensation. This may help to deal with the fairness issue, that is, the objectionableness of imposing charges on people who (perhaps) cannot afford to pay. And a third important reason is that if we focus on the retained benefit, we have a way of assigning responsibility to someone without some deeply questionable idea that guilt is transmitted from generation to generation: Outside theological contexts in which the sin of Adam and Eve is supposed somehow to be transmitted to their progeny, guilt is not something that can be handed down – but profit most certainly is. I can have in my possession a profit that I am not guilty of acquiring. (Suppose someone has led a blameless life – pacific, egalitarian and vegetarian – but that their great-great grandfather, whose ivory collection they have unexpectedly inherited, was an out-and-out scoundrel and an elephant poacher?) As we shall see, this feature of the argument also allows advocates of redress to draw upon an insufficiently well-known but intriguing branch of private law, that of 'Unjust Enrichment', that has played an important role in recent movements for redress in the United States, raising interesting issues of an ethical kind.

Does anyone benefit?

Before we launch into these questions, though, let us first note an apparently basic limitation on the scope of the 'who benefits' line of argument. All atrocities, by definition, involve great loss. Not all produce a great profit, however. Some produce no profit at all, or not, anyway, one that endures. Some examples that come to mind immediately: In 1685, the King of France, Louis XIV, withdrew from his country's Protestant community the limited toleration that it had been granted a century or so before. Thousands of French Protestants (Huguenots), refusing to convert to Catholicism, were killed or forced into exile, and since – as is often the case with religious minorities – they had valuable skills that were under-represented in the majority population, the economic cost to France was great. It was the Protestant countries that received the Huguenot exiles that benefited from the industrial and commercial expertise that they brought with them. Another example: The kingdom of Portugal was at the forefront of Europe's colonial expansion, and at one point had extensive colonial possessions around the world: but at the time of its entry into the European Union, Portugal was among the poorest countries in Europe, qualifying for what we may term the national welfare payments that the richer European countries subsidized. (Among the richest of the European countries providing the cash for the payments, we may note, was Germany, a country with only a minimal and short-lived colonial history.) It is true that, qualifying this point, particular institutions may have benefited even though the atrocity as a whole produced no net benefit to the larger society. The Holocaust produced no net benefit to Germany, quite the reverse, in fact – it produced a devastating loss: but all the same, particular institutions (such as industrial corporations or banks) may have gained and retained a profit from slave labour, and, as we have already seen, some portion of the profits has sometimes been successfully claimed back from them. That qualification aside, though, it is important to make the point that atrocity is not *in general* a reliably profitable business, and is often in fact self-destructive, so that an approach based on 'who benefits' cannot give us a general or all-encompassing view about how to respond. 'Who benefits' may sometimes give us a thread that leads us back, through the causal maze, to the original wrong, but benefiting cannot replace wrongdoing as the paradigm of responsibility, without abandoning too much of the field that advocates of redress want to be covered.

But some atrocities have, at least apparently, given their perpetrators and their descendants some long-term benefits, and so even though the 'who benefits' approach is not comprehensive, it may still be powerful within its own proper range – perhaps more compelling than the alternative approaches that we might bring to bear. And as we have just seen, it has advantages. Those advantages are especially clear in connection with a problem that is sometimes thought to be fatal to the idea that countries owe redress to anyone: the problem of the liability of immigrants. Suppose we could somehow manage to show that responsibility for the ancestors' misdeeds fell to their descendants: What are we then to make of the fact that so many of the inhabitants of most Western societies (a majority of their inhabitants, in some cases) are not descendants of those who committed the misdeeds, but belong to the societies in question because of the enormous waves of migration that took place in the nineteenth and twentieth centuries? The benefits-received view is very well placed to deal with this objection. For it derives liability not from anything that some precursor did, but from the enjoyment of benefits that flow from what was done, and those who subsequently immigrated (or whose ancestors subsequently immigrated) to prosperous Western societies obviously share in those benefits just as those who descend from the eighteenth-century exploiters do, even if not always to the same extent. In fact, if one really wanted to push this point, subsequent immigrants and their descendants may be *more* liable for redress, since in some sense their membership is traceable to a voluntary choice to be a part of a more prosperous society, while the descendants of eighteenth-century settlers have made no sort of choice about what to inherit.

So let us assess the 'who benefits' view. There are four important general issues. The first issue that needs discussion is whether or not it is a good idea to make redress depend on clear demonstrations of benefit, if it is the case that demonstrations of that kind are unlikely always to be clear enough to motivate people to act, or to be safe from basic objections.

The second issue is about what follows from receiving a benefit, if indeed it is clear that, in some case, a benefit *has* been received. This topic has a very long history. In one of the first close discussions of what we owe to others, Plato, in the *Crito* dialogue, put forward the view that receiving benefits creates indebtedness to our benefactors in a very far-reaching way – so far-reaching, in fact, that it obliges us to sacrifice our most basic interests, in recompense.

The third issue is about whether or not the idea of cancelling a benefit captures well enough the nature of the injustice that we want to take account of. And here it is useful to take up the topic mentioned above, that of 'Unjust Enrichment' as a branch of law whose resources advocates of redress have ingeniously exploited, and which, beyond whatever strictly legal merits it may have, offers to make sense of redress from an ethical point of view.

The fourth issue is about what necessarily follows if we decide that what is basically objectionable about wrongdoing is that someone gets to benefit from it. For if that – precisely *that* – is what is objectionable, we can imagine various ways in which that objectionable outcome could be cancelled out in some significant sense – various ways that do not involve redress at all.

Let us look at these issues in turn.

Does injustice pay?

That question may seem to answer itself. Of course it does, disturbingly often. Very possibly, it is true, it has bad psychic consequences for those who perpetrate it, by deforming their sense of value and disordering their judgements of priority – the theme of Plato's *Republic*, a work that is a sustained answer to this very question. Some may hope that Plato was right and that villains do really live in private hells (even if they inhabit luxurious mansions). But that is not usually what is at issue when the blunt language of 'paying' is used. Some jobs deform those who perform them, after all, but they are still called 'paying work', and it is in this simple and materialistic way that the question needs to be understood. Did those who perpetrated injustice profit materially from it? And are those profits now in the hands of their successors? If the answer is 'yes' to both those questions, then the benefit-based case for redress can at least get off the ground.

There are debates about both slavery and colonialism that bear on this. They are complex and involve both empirical evidence and issues about its proper interpretation. For obvious reasons, I will not try to summarize these debates, still less try to adjudicate them. But a little needs to be said about them in order to support a general point that is both true and important. The point is this. The *harm* done by both slavery and colonialism is both immense and undeniable. Any history of either of those topics will contain details of cruelty that will disgust you. The case for redress, however we formulate it, and whatever it leads to, should rest, surely, on that. The *benefits received* (and retained) from slavery and colonialism are very much harder to establish clearly, in a way that evades some very common sceptical objections. First, I will explain why. Second, I will explain why an important philosophical objection to redress does not apply in the case of harm that was done, while it does apply in the case of benefits that were received.

So, first: Why is it hard to establish that slavery and colonialism generated (lasting) benefits for those who perpetrated them? It should, at first sight, be simple enough. After all, the owners of slaves extracted from them millions of person-hours of unpaid but productive work, enabling them to generate profit from (especially) the raw materials that the slave economy supplied to the industrializing economies. And colonialism gave Europeans the power to extract raw materials, from African and Asian countries, that fuelled their own economic success. Now no one is going to deny that particular individuals or companies or cities derived huge profits in this way. But can we say that the existing North American and European societies – those societies on whose governments demands for redress are, for the most part, made – enjoy and retain a benefit?

Certainly there are theories that say that they do. Here are remarks by two advocates of reparations for slavery: 'The resources and labor from the African continent permitted the North to develop and take the lead on Africa,' and 'Africa invested so that the West could become what it is today.'[2] And here are two remarks on the need to compensate the victims of colonialism: 'During colonization . . . raw materials were carried from Africa and used in developing the Western countries,' and 'They come, they tell you "Close your eyes: we baptize you in the name of the Lord the Father"; they take our diamonds away.'[3] In the case of colonialism, of course, there is also a more recent history, and direct victims and beneficiaries of colonization live today. There is also the important matter of neocolonial exploitation, which is made possible by the inferior bargaining position of former colonies. Both of those topics fall outside the scope of this book, because they are not matters of *historical* redress but of simple justice. In the latter case, they involve political and economic arrangements that are ongoing today, and the basis for a demand for remedy is (in my view[4]) absolutely clear. But to the extent that the demand for remedy is based on claims about Western economic development in the eighteenth and nineteenth centuries, the picture gets very much foggier.

Just why take-off happened in Britain and in other European countries, in the later eighteenth and early nineteenth centuries, is among the oldest and most contested questions in economic history. Marx's statement that 'the commercial hunting of black skins' signalled 'the dawn of the era of capitalist production'[5] is sometimes quoted in support of the formative contribution of slavery to economic development; returned to its context, though, it is only one of a number of factors acknowledged by Marx (although he gives it rhetorical prominence): The slave trade was preceded by far-reaching domestic changes that put an end to the feudal system of production (changes which, incidentally, also had many domestic victims, due to 'the expropriation and partial eviction of the country population'[6]). To mention the other great nineteenth-century meta-narrative, Max Weber, as is well known, discovered the roots of the capitalist system in the moral and psychological tensions of the Protestant mind, driven to the work ethic by a desire for a sign of 'election' for salvation. On a broader canvas still, a widely read recent view looks to geography rather than to economics or religion or psychology: Western Europe was favoured in many ways by its climatic situation and its lucky endowment of usable animals, and in the last resort, on that theory, the deep reasons for its economic pre-eminence may predate anything that Western Europeans did, to anyone.[7]

Without getting into far-reaching speculations of this kind, however, detailed evidence-based research suggests that we should be cautious about giving priority to any one factor; that while Western countries derived economic benefits from slavery and colonialism, claims about the decisiveness of their contribution cannot be proved; and that there is no realistic possibility of sorting out how much of the West's economic advance can be traced to slavery or colonialism.[8] An additional level of complexity would be added if we had to establish how much of any benefit has been retained in the present. For in some cases (Portugal was mentioned above), any benefit traceable to colonization has long gone, while in other cases, successive waves of economic change have had such profound effects that what is due to any single factor cannot be reliably figured out. Even if we could be sure that, at a certain point, some quantity of capital could be attributed to the slave trade alone, that capital would later have been put to various uses, some profitable, some not so. Would we count only the profitable uses, so that the benefit could be said to endure and multiply? And if so, would the *un*profitable uses (there have been many!) cancel out the initial benefit, so that its initial extraction would no longer be the basis for a possible claim? That does not seem to be an outcome that advocates of redress should welcome, but if redress is to track the exploiter's profits, it is hard to see why, logically, it should not have to track the exploiter's losses too – if indeed the argument is truly benefit-*based*, that is, based on what someone or other now *has* in his or her possession.

Baseline issues

As mentioned, though, over and above these very briefly sketched sorts of historical issues, there is also a philosophical problem. It is a benchmark or baseline problem, and it stands in the way of any straightforward idea of measuring changes in well-being over a longish period, and especially over generations. For if we want to claim that someone's well-being has been reduced (in the case of harms) or increased (in the case of benefits), we have to say: reduced or increased in relation to *what*? For loss and benefit are comparative notions in the sense that they both involve movement away from some baseline. You lose something because, at the baseline moment, you had it, and you benefit from something because, at the baseline moment, you wanted or needed it. So, what is the right baseline? This is a troublesome issue in the context of global justice. We want to be able to assess the losses and benefits that have arisen, for the developed world and for the South, as a result of the emergence of a global economy. Do we take as our baseline the way both parts of the world were in the eighteenth century? Or do we make guesses about where they would be now, if no global economy had come into being? The former seems artificial. As for the latter, 'we must plead complete ignorance', one commentator has said.[9] In the case of justice between generations, the difficulties are at least as troublesome as in the case of global justice, perhaps even more so. Don't we have to plead ignorance in this case too?

Let us take the case of harm first. We may say that someone has been harmed by some past event, meaning that the person thus harmed is worse off than the same person unharmed. Suppose, though, that but for that past event, the person in question would not have existed, so that there is no such person as 'the same person, but unharmed'? How can we say that *they* have been harmed by an event but for which *they* would not even be an entity capable of being harmed, or benefited, by anything? Imagine, borrowing a philosopher's useful micro-example,[10] that a generation or two ago, person X dug an asbestos mine. It was productive, and a small town sprang up around the mine to house and service the miners. Two people came from elsewhere to work in the mine, met, married and had children. Eventually, their children contracted asbestosis, a fatal lung disease. If they make a claim against person X, cannot person X say, in response to their claim: Were it not for me, and the mining project that I founded, you would not even exist, with or without asbestosis. Asbestosis is certainly bad, but what is it *worse* than? There is not, as it were, a you without asbestosis who would lead a better life than you do with asbestosis, because you and your asbestosis result from exactly the same process. We may take the point one cruel step further. The same process that produced your asbestosis also gave you the benefit of existence. Is living, with asbestosis, worse than not living at all?

The same kind of issue is posed by claims about benefits to the perpetrators and their descendants. You could do something that would bring you some financial return, but whether or not it would be 'to your benefit' would surely depend, for a baseline, on what opportunities you had to forgo in order to do it. You could, for example, take on a paper route, getting up before dawn every day, delivering 30 or 40 morning papers, and earning $7 a week. But suppose this took so much out of you that you had no energy for your sought-after and highly profitable talent for cutting-edge performance art, for which galleries would pay you thousands? Then the paper route would not be 'to your benefit'. As in the case of measuring harm, we need a baseline so that we can make comparative judgements. People benefit, just as they lose, in relation to something else that might have happened instead.

Now what-might-have-been always involves some element of speculation, of course, and so we might feel we are being led here to the conclusion that talk about harm or benefit is inherently unreliable and subjective, involving such unknowable factors that it is better to avoid it altogether. But in the case of harm (though not of benefit), there is a good answer to this worry about speculativeness. It is true that it may seem odd to say that X, the asbestos-mine entrepreneur, is accountable for harming *you*, the asbestosis victim, given that it was his business enterprise that brought *you* into existence in the first place (so that there is no 'unharmed you', so to speak, that the life of 'harmed you' is worse than). But if someone has a general duty, it applies to anyone who comes within its scope. If someone has a general duty not to expose others to lethal danger, it applies to anyone who is led to incur the danger.[11] The duty is not specifically to you, it is to anyone who falls within a certain type[12] or class, in this case, the class of people living in close proximity to asbestos dust. Your personal history is neither here nor there. Perhaps it *is* the case that your parents were asbestos workers (so that you would not have existed but for the mine). But you might have been a stray child who was taken in by kindly asbestos workers. Or you might have been sent away every summer to spend holidays with your aunt and uncle, the nice asbestos workers. Or you might have spent time in the mining community for some quite extraneous reason, such as an interest in local fossils or butterflies. It does not matter. Whatever moral liability falls to the asbestos mine does not depend on the particular histories of those exposed to its danger, but on the common fact of their exposure to it.

So, widening the scope quite a bit, we may have an answer to those who object to African-American demands for slavery reparations on the grounds that, but for slavery, no African-Americans would exist. The answer is that those who conducted the monstrous slavery enterprise violated a duty to all those likely to be harmed by it. That class of people obviously includes, and very prominently, the children of slaves, who, it is quite true, would not be who they were but for slavery: but how they came to be who they are is, for the purpose of establishing moral liability, not the point. The descendants of slaves are those who are most likely to fall into the class of people who are harmed by a predictably harmful policy of massive inhumanity.

We have arguments, then, that may be able to rescue the 'harm' argument from the baseline problem. But, getting back to the issue of 'benefits', there seems to be no parallel argument here. Slave owners and colonialists did wrong in many, many ways, and that, to repeat, is why we need to take the idea of redress seriously. But they did no wrong in seeking benefits, a purpose that, in itself, involves no violation of a duty that brings into play a type or class of claimant. Causing harm (to anyone who suffers it) is wrong. Seeking a benefit is not, and that someone in the past sought a benefit does not transmit obligations to the future in the same way. Harm essentially taints, benefits do not.

WHO BENEFITS? 51

Would the fact that they received benefits add something to the case against them, however, if it could be shown that they gained more from slavery and/or colonialism than they could have gained from any other available policies – and, moreover, that those surplus gains remained in the hands of their successors? That would complicate matters – we could say that in that case, the benefits were *uniquely* traceable to exploitation, that they could not have been got by some other means – but it seems unlikely that it can be shown in a decisive enough way. We just do not know how the southern states of the United States would have fared economically if at some point (when?) they had adopted a system of wage labour instead of slavery. We just do not know how imperial powers (such as Britain) would have fared economically if (when?) instead of treating colonies as suppliers of raw material, they had encouraged their economic development and then enjoyed privileged access to developing consumer markets. My point: Do we really want to make the case for historical redress depend on questions like this? Would the case for redress for slavery really evaporate if our best historians told us that, in the long term, and fully costed out, it was a dreadful idea not just morally, but economically too? And does the case against colonialism really turn on showing that, right now, former colonial powers enjoy a standard of living that they would not otherwise enjoy – so that if they did not, if their wealth were to be wiped out by some financial disaster, we could forget about the colonial past altogether?

It is easy, but mistaken, to slip back, at this point, into an argument that is really about remedying a loss. In reply to the objection described just above, someone could say: It really does not matter that the exploiters got less benefit, or as much benefit, or more benefit from slavery or colonialism than they could have got from some other line of activity. The point is that they got *these* benefits in *that* way, and the benefits that they actually got, not hypothetical benefits that they might have got in some other way, were wrongly taken, and remain in their successors' hands. But this shifts the argument back to what the victims of slavery or colonialism lost, and the wrong that was done in exploiting them. And that loss and that wrong would create a moral burden whether the exploiters benefited at all, not to mention the still more complicated question of whether those benefits continue to be in someone's hands. The message, then, of this part of the discussion is: Surely it is best not to use complicated and hard-to-prove arguments when simple ones have a chance of doing rather better.

Do benefits create duties?

According to Plato, when Socrates was awaiting execution (he had been convicted of subversive teaching), he was visited by a friend, Crito, an influential man who had the means to spring Socrates from prison and to convey him to another city where he could live out his life unharmed. Instead of having to drink the fatal hemlock, he was offered a chance to spend his remaining years on a rocking-chair on some pleasant shady foreign porch, perhaps dialoguing playfully with admirers, as he so much liked to do. In Plato's account of the conversation that followed, Socrates rejected Crito's well-meant offer on a variety of grounds, all of which have been extensively discussed by political philosophers. For our purposes, the one that matters is the idea of *benefit*. Plato has Socrates say that his city, Athens, could claim to have given him his life ('Was it not through us that your father married your mother and begot you?') and his education ('Are you not grateful [for laws] . . . requiring your father to give you a cultural and physical education?'). On this line of argument, having received a benefit is a powerful reason to do something in return. (Even to die at the benefactor's request, according to the *Crito*, a dialogue that certainly has the merit of going as far as the argument takes it.)

But in recent thinking, this tends to be regarded as a somewhat sketchy argument, thanks in large part to a counter-example devised by one of the twentieth century's most ingenious political philosophers.[13] Suppose, in your neighbourhood, a group of people get together and broadcast a mix of music and interesting news items through powerful loudspeakers, so that everyone within a certain range can hear. You are among those who can hear, and you quite enjoy the music and current-events trivia that have been made available to you. And then one day one of the neighbourhood entertainment activists comes to your door and says brightly: 'Your turn now! Tomorrow's programming duty is down to you!' Having benefited, do you now have to contribute?

Well, among the main reasons why you should not have to contribute is that the enjoyment that you get from the local broadcast system, even though is significant, may not be enough to make you think it worthwhile to make the effort to contribute. Of course, you may just be a shameless free rider: Really you love the broadcasts and plan your whole day around them, but, being smart, you have figured out that they will happen anyway, whether you contribute or not. Then morality condemns you as a mean person, or perhaps as an economist. (Mean persons and economists are both wedded to the idea of rational self-interest.) But it is always possible that while you enjoy the amenity, your enjoyment is below the threshold that would motivate you to spend the time to contribute to it, at the expense of some other activity that is above the threshold – origami, let us say. While you quite like having the amenity, you would rather do without it if you had to spend time on supporting it rather than making small paper sculptures. It will of course be hard to tell, without divine insight into people's souls, whether any given person was a free rider (thus morally bad) or a below-threshold supporter (thus morally acceptable). And it is quite true – as critics of the public broadcast scenario have maintained – that many valuable public goods would not get to be supplied at all if we had to prove that unwilling contributors were free riders (who want them) rather than below-threshold supporters (who do not want them enough).[14] But all that shows, I believe, is that supplying valuable public goods should not be based on the you-like-it-so-you-pay-for-it basis. We need to find less dubious ways – some of which, by the way, are also pointed to by the *Crito* dialogue, but following those up here would take us too far afield. The point, for now, is simply that having received a benefit from some past event does not seem to lead us straight to an obligation to make up for the loss or the cost that the past event involved. The point is of course even stronger when the benefit is not one that arises from any sort of action of your own – in the case of the public broadcasts, you may perhaps have opened the windows in order to hear them better, or even purchased some sort of sound-amplifying equipment such as a hearing aid – but, as in the case at hand, from an inheritance that you never even sought.

But even if the receipt-of-benefits argument is not as convincing as it needs to be, perhaps another step can save it. That you have inherited something may bring into play a further consideration, mentioned briefly above: one that concerns ability to pay. We cannot ever say that people ought to do things that they literally cannot do – 'ought implies can' is the concise formula that is often used to sum up this idea – and not having the resources to meet some demand is certainly a good reason to decline it. There are all sorts of reasons why you may want to decline a panhandler's moving plea for a hand-out, for example, but among those reasons having no money to give would be pretty decisive. Now, that one enjoys a benefit – and so has resources at one's disposal – would seem to rule out that kind of reason for refusing to aid. But does it really? That would seem to depend, surely, on what has been done with the benefit, and on the place that it has come to assume in the owners' (and others') lives. Whole civilizations have been built on land seized from indigenous peoples. Profits from slavery have been invested in important and valuable projects. Millions of people, in former colonizing countries, live lives that in one way or another are shaped by the colonial past. Of course, facts like that do not simply speak for themselves. We need a view that enables us to see what practical implications follow. But here is one such view that we have to consider. Suppose we say that what underpins the idea of property is that it enables people to build their lives around secure expectations, so that they can carry out the ordinary basic tasks of human life, those of forming plans and relationships that depend on

WHO BENEFITS?

predictable knowledge of what is theirs and what is not. If we take that view, we will want to give a great deal of weight to what it is that, as a matter of fact, people have built their expectations around.[15] And harsh as this conclusion may sound – or, more honestly put, harsh as it may actually be – on such a view present expectations generally trump lapsed ones. Present possession gives rise to legitimate expectations. The circumstances of past possession do not (whatever else they may give rise to).

Moreover, even if we take a hard line and refuse to be impressed by that sort of excuse, it would not follow that the possession of some resource created a duty to apply it to some particular purpose. That would require another argument altogether. We might say that if there is some sort of undeserved deprivation, then whoever has the resources to correct it should respond. That is the essential point of the story of the Good Samaritan – being on the spot, and having the means to pay for a night in the inn, the Good Samaritan has a duty to look after the injured man in the roadway. But the whole point of that parable is that the Samaritan has no connection with the victim at all – he is from Samaria. Others, with a nearer connection to the victim, pass by, but the Samaritan does not: that, after all, is why he is a Good one. He is good without regard to any special connections created by kinship or nationality or past relationships. Exactly for that reason, the ability-to-help argument is not going to persuade people that they have some special reason to aid others on the basis of some historical relationship of exploitation. If they follow the example of the Good Samaritan, they will, if truly good, look around for the neediest person to help, regardless of their connection with them. (Or perhaps the person most likely to benefit from help.) That person may or may not be a descendant of those groups from whom our ancestors extracted the benefits that we now possess. That person – to borrow an example from the previous chapter – may be a refugee who has suffered persecution in which neither we nor our ancestors had any hand at all, but whose plight is dire and whose needs are of a kind that we can effectively meet.

So, for both of those reasons, we should not adopt that way of rescuing the receipt-of-benefits argument. First, it is true that enjoying a benefit gives you resources: but we have to take account of the place that those resources have come to occupy in an ongoing way of life, and second, if – like the Good Samaritan – we have disposable resources, we may be more strongly moved by claims of need than by claims based on some personal or historical connection, and so decide to use our resources accordingly, at the expense of historical redress.

Unjust Enrichment

But here is a quite different line of thinking. You go to the bank to cash a cheque for $101. The teller is tired (it is late in the day on Friday) and thinks it is a cheque for $110. She gives you $110, you go home, and some time later you realize what has happened: you have $9 more than you should have. If you are like me, or like any other person I have ever met, you (1) may briefly wonder if you should return the money and then (2) conclude that you should not. If you are like me, or like any other person I have ever met, the fact that the bank – let us call it the Imperial Bank of the Cosmos (IBC) – has incalculably larger resources than you will play a part in this decision. (Getting the wrong change from a corner store owned by a recent immigrant, living off tight profit margins, would probably, I hope, lead to a different result.) So, return the $9? Not likely. – Wrong answer. The law, in common-law countries such as the United States, the United Kingdom and Canada, clearly says: Return it. If you do not, the IBC can get it back from you.

That answer is given to us by a branch of law called the law of Unjust Enrichment, which is particularly relevant from the point of view of this chapter because it does not depend on the idea of fault. You did not commit any fault when you walked out of the IBC with an extra $9. No blame attaches to you. You did not lie or cheat or steal, or try to distract the teller by making unusual noises or using hypnotic suggestion. But for as long as you remain in possession of the $9, you have benefited from an unjust transaction, and although you may see no reason why you should give it back to IBC, nor, however, can you give a reason why, in justice, you should retain it. Before we move on to discuss the interesting implications for historical redress, let us just note two things that will turn out to be important: (1) in receiving the benefit you did nothing wrong, and (2) nevertheless you can give no reason in justice why you should retain it. They are crucial to the discussion that follows.

In the United States, actions under the law of Unjust Enrichment have involved, once again, the case of slavery. We can at once see how (1) immediately above comes into play. Present generations did not enslave anyone. That fact stands in the way of imposing on them any sort of reparative duty based on what their ancestors did. But if present generations benefit from what their ancestors did, then we do not have to show that present generations did anything wrong. We just have to make a case for their giving up the benefit that remains in their hands. At once, then, as we have seen, there is the possibility of setting aside one of the most basic objections to historical redress – that guilt is not inheritable, because it can arise only from what you yourself have done. Unjust Enrichment is not about what you have done, it is about what you have.

That line of thinking has been adopted in several important and ethically provocative legal actions that bring the benefit-based approach into sharp focus. One in particular is a protracted lawsuit against Aetna (an insurance company), and other US corporations, that began as a class action suit in a court in Brooklyn, New York, in 2002. The prominent lawyers who crafted this suit based it on the claim that Aetna and the other corporations named had benefited from the unpaid labour of slaves in the pre-Civil War period, in Aetna's case by selling (and profiting from) the insurance policies that slave owners took out on their human property. The suit sought the return of these profits in the form of a cash settlement to be made to the descendants of slaves. Eventually, as the suit came to be consolidated with other suits of a similar kind, additional claims were added; for example, that the corporations continued to benefit, fraudulently, from their history, in that consumers with a social conscience were more willing to purchase their products to the extent that the corporations concealed their unpleasant historical taint.

Now of course, people who advocate important causes are surely free to use whatever instruments come to hand. This interesting branch of law is among them, and its use has successfully helped to bring publicity to the evil of slavery. But law is one thing, morality another, and so one can always ask if what the law expresses is what morality wants us to say. And here the use of Unjust-Enrichment law meets a serious objection. It is true that unpaid labour was extracted from slaves. Unjust-Enrichment law gives ingenious advocates a grip on the evil of that extraction. But is that really why slavery was evil? Surely that is only one among its many evils, and to focus on its remedy is to risk placing the real history of slavery, a history that expresses the slaves' own experience, in the margin.[16] That line of criticism has all the more force as we move to the secondary benefits of slavery, such as the possession of profits made by companies that were not themselves slave owners, but that made money out of slavery by (for example) selling insurance policies, and whose commercial reputation benefits from the concealment of that fact. That seems to move us rather too far away from the centre of the moral point. But even if we stick with the much less tenuously related issue of unpaid labour, the objection that the point has been missed still remains to be considered.

Now on the face of the matter, this objection is a very telling one, if we bear in mind the original example that launched this discussion. You can be unjustly enriched even if you have done nothing wrong, because the benefit that you received may have been the result of, say, a bank teller's inadvertence. The point is that you had no right to receive it, not that you did wrong in getting it. And so it may seem odd to put the model of unjust enrichment to use as a weapon against slavery – for if those who enslaved people did not commit a wrong, then it is hard to think of anything that *would* amount to committing a wrong, and a model that avoids the issue of moral blame seems exactly to miss the point. People were not inadvertently enslaved, after all, in the way that our bank customer was inadvertently enriched. Against this view, however, a subtle and important consideration must be weighed.[17]

It is true that what we may call the point or the purpose, in the model of unjust enrichment, is not to place blame or right a wrong but to reverse a transfer that should not have happened. But in the case of slavery, the transfer is unjust, thus requiring reversal, only because slavery was a wrong: The benefits that some institutions now hold are unjustly held because the manner in which they were transferred can no longer be given a shred of moral defence. So even though the essential point or the defining purpose is not to right a wrong or to place blame somewhere, the wrongness of slavery is fundamentally implied. It is the necessary link that makes it possible to challenge present holdings in light of past events. And because what is challenged is the retention of a benefit, what matters is whether enslaved labour is justifiable *now*, not what (racist) views may have been held by some at the time of its enslavement. So this approach gives us a particularly sharp and consistent answer to the problems that are set by changing values. It does not matter that some people might have thought slavery was justified 200 years ago, because (they claimed) Africans had no souls: What matters is whether those who now hold its benefits can now justify their retention.

Moreover – the advocate of this view rightly points out – the wrong of unpaid labour epitomizes the nature of slavery. It is true that, taken literally, the non-payment of labour hardly captures the whole brutal injustice of slavery: but it stands for the idea, itself at the core of slavery, that one person can be the property of another and does not even qualify for the minimal notion of human equality that is acknowledged in the wage relationship, which involves the purchase of something belonging to the labourer rather than the purchase of the labourers themselves. Even Marx, who occasionally played with the idea that being a wage-earner was like being a slave, noted the basic difference between the slave's counting for nothing at all and the wage-earner's counting for something. In *Capital*, he wrote:

> The continuance of [the wage] relation demands that the owner of the labour-power should sell it only for a definite period, for if he were to sell it rump and stump, once for all, he would be selling himself, converting himself from a free man into a slave, from an owner of a commodity into a commodity.[18]

That difference – between counting for nothing at all and counting at least for something – is captured by the demand that the extraction of unpaid labour be redressed. The demand thus strikes at what we may see as the most basic evil of slavery. In that way (at least some) legal actions under the Unjust Enrichment model do not, in the last resort, miss the moral point at all: On the contrary, they express it very powerfully.

Faced with those two opposed but well-articulated views, I favour the second. It may say something not altogether good about a society that demands for justice, if they are to succeed, have to be framed in ways that law can accommodate. What is wrong with appealing to justice itself? But the second view shows us that the Unjust Enrichment model should not be seen only as an ingenious legal resource in a litigious society, but that it also has an important expressive meaning. To demand to be paid may seem too minimal a demand, certainly, but to be recognized as a bearer of interests, not as an item of property, is essential to human dignity.

That said, however, we still cannot conclude that the Unjust Enrichment model can help us with the basic task of this chapter, or of this book. For, as just noted, the idea that current holdings are unjust clearly *draws upon* our sense that, whatever justifications may have been available at the time, the ownership of one human by another cannot be right. Bringing an action for unpaid labour (or even for profits tainted by it) may also be a way of *expressing* the wrong in a way that is public, and that has real consequences that testify to its seriousness.

But just because of this, the return-of-benefits model cannot give us a *basic* approach. On a subtle and sympathetic view, it gives us a way of highlighting past injustice and compelling action in response to it. Why we should want to do that, however, still needs to be explained. Why is it important that past injustice should be recalled and remedied? We may say that a way of remedying it – such as an action in Unjust Enrichment – can be compellingly advocated as a way of recalling it. But don't we then have to face another 'that was then' objection? We seem to have gone round in a bit of a circle. Our first question was about why past injustice should matter to us. In this chapter, we have considered the view that we should care about it because some continue to enjoy its benefits. But then it turned out that the best reason for withdrawing those benefits from those who now hold them is that it is a good way of persuading people to recall past injustice. So, back to square one – why does past injustice need to be recalled?

Is redress the right response?

Our fourth and last issue, in this chapter, is about whether or not the continuing existence of a benefit in someone's hands necessarily leads us to a policy of redress, as opposed to some other kind of response. We may find it really objectionable that someone enjoys benefits that can be traced to some past injustice, but, all the same, not decide that we need to turn to redress as the remedy. For example, an insurance company or a college that had received the profits of slavery could simply dispose of them somehow – throw them away. (This is, needless to say, a hypothetical rather than a practical thought.) Or it could give the benefits to a cause or charity entirely unconnected with the descendants of the groups from whom the benefits were originally derived. Here is a real-world parallel: Cecil Rhodes, a thoroughly objectionable arch-imperialist whose fortune derived largely from what we would now call blood diamonds, endowed a Trust (the Rhodes Trust) that generously supports some 80 Commonwealth students for study in the United Kingdom. When they are interviewed for the Rhodes Scholarship, progressively minded students – whose views are at the opposite end of the spectrum from imperialistic ones – regularly say that they want to put Cecil Rhodes's legacy (and money) to uses that are quite different from Rhodes's own purposes, and, moreover, that doing so may help to make up to some degree for the harm that Rhodes himself did in acquiring his fortune. No doubt that view is motivated in part by the astute applicants' personal ambition. But is anything wrong with it? Accepting a Rhodes Scholarship would not contribute to the current trade in blood diamonds, after all, and may in the long run enable good ends to be pursued, ends that are all the more admirable the more they would have dismayed Rhodes himself or (even better?) goaded him into fury.

Vaporizing the benefit, giving it away, putting it to a use that tends to make up for the harm arising from its creation – any of those things would tend to cancel the benefit no less effectively than its return to a descendant of (or proxy for) the group from whom the benefit was once extracted. Perhaps much more effectively, sometimes. And if we continue to think it is important that the benefit should not just be removed from the beneficiary's possession but actually returned to whoever it was that originally lost it (or a proxy for whoever that was), is it still the possession of the benefit that really matters to us, or, rather – as the last chapter discussed – the continued suffering of a loss? Is the argument from benefits received really just a detour?

In the Introduction, mention was made of the effort, in the past half-century, to bring atrocious acts within the scope of criminal law. After a long hiatus, the 1945 Nuremberg Tribunal was succeeded by the special courts for (the former) Yugoslavia and for Rwanda, and then by the International Criminal Court whose jurisdiction is accepted by most nations (although not by some of the most powerful). Criminal law, as the Introduction also mentioned, differs from redress in that its aim is to inflict some sort of damage on the offender rather than to confer some sort of compensation on the offender's victim. But among the most persuasive justifications for criminal law is that it responds to the idea of *unfair benefit*. Whatever else it does – maybe it deters future violations, maybe it does not; probably it does not – criminal law strikes at the benefits of crime. The violator, on one compelling view, claims a sort of illegitimate privilege. When he takes my mountain bike and puts it to his use, he is implicitly claiming that his interest in the use of the bike is weightier than my own, hence (generalizing somewhat) that his interests are weightier than mine, and hence (generalizing even further) that he is in some way worthier than I am. He diminishes me, comparatively. That implication is obviously inconsistent with our common membership in a community in which we enjoy equal status as fellow citizens. I cannot have equal civil status with someone who believes that his interests count for so much that mine count for nothing. So if he is caught and punished, we can best think of his punishment as a practical denial of his implied claim to privilege. By deducting something from *his* interests – his interests in liberty, say, or property, or reputation[19] – punishment restores the equality of status that his crime has implicitly denied. It reaffirms the status of the victim.[20]

All this bears on the question of whether the possession of a benefit necessarily gives us a moral basis for, specifically, a policy of making redress. If the possession of the benefit can be cancelled out in some other way – by deducting, by means of punishment, some notionally equivalent thing from the things enjoyed by the perpetrator – then there isn't any necessary link between benefit and redress; and – to repeat an earlier point – if we think it is important not just that the benefit be cancelled but that some particular person or body should get it back then we cannot be following a benefit-*based* argument for redress. We must have something else in mind, something that requires not just that the benefit's holder should *lose* it but that some particular person or group should *get* it instead. The following chapters continue our search for what that reason might be. Meanwhile, I think we have to say that, on reflection, and despite its promise, the benefit-based approach does not get us where we need to go.

3
WHAT MEMORY CALLS FOR

This chapter discusses yet another approach. So far, we have looked at the survival of rights and at the continuing enjoyment of benefits, as reasons for redress. But for some theorists of redress, neither of those approaches captures what is important. For both of those approaches focus, in their different but complementary ways, on some object that is lost by someone and gained by another, picking out either the loss (Chapter 1) or the gain (Chapter 2) as the ethically central feature and as the basis for making redress. But what is important may not be the object that is lost or gained, but the event or process through which the loss and gain took place; and what is primarily called for in response to that, some critics say, is *memory* of what occurred, rather than the cancellation of the loss or gain that it led to. Of course, approaches can be combined, and in practice one does not exclude another – cancelling the loss or the gain may be a very good way of commemorating the wrongful process: but we are in search of the basic argument for redress, and 'memory' offers a quite different (and undeniably important) starting-point.

In the simplest sense of that word you can be said to 'remember' some event if it is in your mind or if you can call it to mind without having to Google it. I can remember, say, the PIN for my bank account and so can manage to withdraw money from the ATM. In that sense, it may at first, at least, seem a bit odd to say that one can have a duty to remember something. Either it is in your mind or it is not. It is just a matter of fact. Certainly it is a good thing to remember some things (such as PINs), but are you actually at fault, in a moral sense, if you cannot? For it is also good that we forget some things, as philosophers (following Nietzsche) have pointed out: There is a limited space in our personal consciousness and we can function only if some things get deleted from it. If not, we are simply overwhelmed. There is a story by Borges about this ('Funes the Memorious'). And as one American neuroscientist has asked: 'Do you really want to remember all the faces you saw on the New York City subway this morning?'[1] The same is true, as was noted briefly in the Introduction, in the case of whole societies, which can be paralysed if too much of the past is always present to them, so that (e.g.) every situation comes to be responded to on the basis of analogy with some traumatic past event.

But even in the case of personal memory, people are as a matter of fact regularly blamed for forgetting things, just as though there were an actual duty to remember them. Important anniversaries such as spouses' birthdays, of course, come to mind at once. ('What can I do that will be remembered for ever and ever?' the joke goes – answer: 'Forget your wife's birthday.') That is because while it is true that either something is in one's mind or is not, there is much more to the whole story than that, and the 'more' is to do, mainly, with paying attention. Sure, I cannot be blamed for the bare fact that some number or date or fact is not in my mind. But I can be blamed if, at some earlier stage, decisions that I have made have had the effect of keeping it out of my mind, decisions that reflect priorities that are questionable or disturbing from some point of view about what I should be paying attention to, given that I have important attachments and commitments.

The philosopher John Locke is famous for the claim that either something is in your mind or it is not, for that view formed part of his influential case for religious toleration.[2] It is pointless to persecute people for not having a belief that you think they should have, he argued, because if they do not already have that belief, then nothing you can do by way of threats will cause them to have it. We believe what we do on the basis of what we see. Maybe you can make people *say* that they have a belief, but that is not what you want, unless you are a hypocritical persecutor, one who is content with insincere lip service. But, causing much damage to this particular argument for toleration, Locke also claimed (elsewhere) that we indirectly control what we come to believe, in part, by deciding what to give our attention to. Not only that, but decisions about what to attend to are powerfully influenced by our desires, so that the world that we come to see is at least in part the one that we want to see. Locke's famous example is that of a man who simply does not want to grasp that the woman he loves is unfaithful to him, so that 'three kind words' from her will prevent the unwelcome evidence from even entering his mind.[3] Before things enter our minds, they are filtered by a mental apparatus in which our desires play a part. So to that extent, it is not true that it is altogether an involuntary matter that some item is in our mind or not. At some point, you may have made decisions that influence whether it is in there or not.

If that is so in the personal case, the same is even more clearly true in the social or political case. In the social or political case, there isn't of course a single collective mind in which some belief or memory can be said to be present or not. Society does not have a mind. An assortment of different beliefs and memories occupy different people's individual minds. At the collective level, there is *only* what we just called an 'apparatus', one that strongly influences what gets into individual minds. What goes into this apparatus is enormously complex. School textbooks come to mind at once; also mass media, and the effects upon it of the political interests of those who own it; cultural presentations of what is normal and what is exceptional; public documents that convey official endorsements of some views while explicitly or implicitly undermining others.

When we switch from the personal to the social or political level, then, we make a switch from 'memory', in its root sense (what is in someone's mind), to what may better be termed 'memorial' – which we may think of as the socially and politically provided apparatus that promotes the formation of some beliefs while obstructing the formation of others. 'Socially and politically' is rather an evasive phrase to use here, because obviously part of the apparatus reproduces prevalent social beliefs while part of it is directly subject to political control, and the distinction between the two is important. But all of it is *ultimately* subject, if not to political control, to political influence at least. In that sense, it is open to deliberate change. The memorial apparatus of a political society is the range of instruments that govern what beliefs are likely to come into its inhabitants' minds, and to ask about 'duties of memory' is to ask about what governments have a duty to do in relation to those beliefs, or what citizens ought to persuade governments that they have a duty to do.

We may divide those duties into two kinds. First, there are said to be duties to maintain the apparatus of memory, or to create it in cases where it does not exist. Second, there are said to be duties to perform public actions that flow from memory, such as (notably) making apologies for past outrages; or, more uncommonly, such things as reburying the remains of someone who was unjustly dishonoured some centuries ago.[4] Clearly, the two kinds overlap: building a museum or erecting a statue, for example, or issuing a commemorative stamp – would count both as contributions to the apparatus of memory and as public actions arising from memory. But some reasons are specific to the two kinds, so let us consider them somewhat separately. In both cases, I shall argue, what we mainly need to consider is whether or not the merits of individual memory or apology can be transferred quite successfully, or without distortion, to the social or political level.

Kinds of memory

We can assume – I hope – that history (meaning here the study and recovery of the past) is a good thing. I am really not at all sure how to support that assumption, beyond asking people who do not share it to consider that the record of what humans have done is part of what we mean by 'humanity', and that if any of it becomes unrecoverable, then our conception of the human is diminished. Some loss seems to take place when something of importance to a human being is irretrievably unrecorded, whether it was important as a triumph or a disaster or a sacrifice. There are also many reasons for believing that history is useful, as a supply of evidence about human nature, as a repertoire of solutions and as a source both of chastening lessons about failed plans and of inspiring models of idealism. All of that needs much further defence, of course, but we need not dwell on it here because, whatever it is that makes history itself important, we need to distinguish 'history' from 'memory', our topic in this chapter.

'Memory', in this context, is not the study of the past, and while it is about the recovery of the past, it is a recovery that is motivated in a particular way. History, too, is of course motivated, in various ways at various times. But memory is motivated by a desire to affirm something about the situation of a society or of a group within it, the values that it embodies, the trials that it has had to endure. When, for example, Protestant groups in Northern Ireland 'remember' the Battle of the Boyne that took place in 1690 – an event that secured the long-term ascendancy of Protestants over Catholics in Ireland – their purpose is not to explore the very interesting geopolitical aspects of the Catholic–Protestant rivalry in seventeenth-century Europe, nor even to re-enact that battle with antique uniforms and authentically unreliable muskets, but to affirm the importance of the event for their present circumstances. It is to make it present in its symbolic meaning, a meaning that recalls particular triumphs, threats overcome, and virtues displayed.[5]

It is important to distinguish between two very different kinds of recovery that memory undertakes. One, which we might call *dis*covery, is concerned with bringing to light factual matters that have been suppressed. It overlaps with (part of) the work of history itself, with the difference, again, that it is driven by the immediate connection of those matters to present circumstances. This is the memorial effort that goes into finding out what happened to the 'disappeared' victims of terror campaigns, to the opening of mass graves to count and if possible identify the bodies, to correcting official lies about what happened to political prisoners who died in prison, and to other

WHAT MEMORY CALLS FOR

activities that are important to people – especially to victims' families and friends – after atrocities have been covertly conducted. Not only is this essential to what psychologists call the work of mourning – the coming-to-terms with loss – it is demanded by the value of truth-telling itself, for it is a response to policies that were concealed by systematic lies and deceptions. If any form of memory is morally required, this is surely it, and of the many things attempted by devices such as truth commissions, this is, deservedly, the least controversial. When memory of this kind is suppressed or passed over, the interesting example of post-Franco Spain suggests, it reasserts itself – a generation after the fall of Franco's fascist dictatorship, despite an initial consensus to let bygones be bygones, the desire to discover what happened to its victims was powerfully revived.

But this is very different from what we may call the memory of 'rehearsal', which is not concerned with finding new facts but, on the contrary, with the repetition of narratives that are well known and have indeed even become formulaic through repetition. This, too, is driven by a sense of the immediate connection between past – or an imagined past – and present. In this mode, memory strongly resembles myth, as long as we bear in mind that myths are not necessarily untrue, but are defined by the way in which they are taken to establish the meaning of present circumstances or activities by recounting some episode, real or not; an episode in which certain kinds of character were displayed, or certain kinds of obstacles were overcome, or certain kinds of enemies were defeated. Romulus and Remus, the mythic founders of Rome (said to have been raised by wolves), surely did not exist. Robin Hood probably existed, but may have been nothing remotely like his portrayal in any of the many movies about him. Lord Nelson certainly did exist, although the stories about him are sure to contain exaggerations and omissions and fictions. All three figure in political memories that have inspired people. Can we ever say that *that* kind of memory is morally required?

Two paragraphs above I chose an initial example that many readers of this book are likely to be out of sympathy with. Celebrating the Battle of the Boyne is a politically charged ritual that is intended to express triumphalist sentiments in an aggressive and divisive way. Other kinds of rehearsal memory – sometimes said to be present in Serbian political culture, for example, or the political culture of Afrikaners[6] – may strain our sympathy for a different reason: They rehearse failures or defeats rather than triumphs, and so feed a political style of suspiciousness and resentment. Obviously, we need to bear all such examples in mind, for if we confine our attention to beneficial examples of memory, we are not actually answering the question at hand. We are just saying that remembrance is good when it leads to results that we favour. And obviously, it is very unsatisfactory to say it is good to remember in those cases in which memory is a good thing, and not good when it is not. But it seems extraordinarily hard to escape that lame conclusion. For what are our alternatives?

It would seem that in evaluating rehearsal-type memories, we have a choice between assessing their truthfulness and assessing their inspirational content. Setting aside Romulus and Remus and their mythic lupine day care, and King Arthur and the Knights of the Round Table, it is probably true that influential memories often have some factual basis, and so do not involve a total fabrication of the past. There really was, after all, an evacuation of British troops at Dunkirk in 1940, and it really did involve some use of small boats, even though – the cold eye of history has shown – the significance of the small boats is exaggerated in the remembered story.[7] We can come to the defence of the remembered story in two ways. We can say that even history, at its very coldest, is necessarily selective, and so there is nothing basically objectionable about the selectiveness of popular memory. There just is no such thing as an unselective account of the Dunkirk evacuation or of anything else at all, and the popular memory picks out what is interesting from a certain point of view, as any record does. Alternatively, we can look to the moral, or the lessons, of the popular account, and defend it on the grounds that it yields a story in which certain virtues such as being 'stubborn, independent . . . [showing] courage in the face of massive adversity'[8] are foregrounded in an inspiring way. Taking that defence a step further, we may even claim for it a kind of truth, 'moral' truth perhaps, if those virtues have in fact sometimes been displayed by British people. The Dunkirk story concretizes them in a compact narrative form, and is important for that reason.

But as soon as we take that second step, factual truth has fled the scene in a big hurry. If moral truth alone is a good test, why not embrace the defence of Romulus and Remus and King Arthur? Romans no doubt found their founding myth inspiring and were better citizens because of it; and even today, entirely non-Roman children might derive respect and liking for wolves and other endangered species from it. The Camelot story may, in the distant past, have inspired chivalrous knightly exploits, some of which may possibly have been good. If moral or inspirational 'truth' is the appropriate validating test for a story, what actually happened is beside the point, and so the fact that the story does or does not have some real representational content is neither here nor there. If that is so, rehearsal-type memories are 'memories' only in a sort of courtesy sense, for surely a memory in any plain sense of that term is a representation of something that really happened. If their representational content is actually irrelevant, then surely it is right to conclude that we should evaluate them in terms of the value of what they teach, rejecting them if (e.g.) they teach xenophobia or hatred, or close off access to important truths, or serve to support hierarchy.[9] If they were offensive in those ways, we should stop rehearsing them even if they were factually true (though we should continue to record their truth). If that is the conclusion that we are led to, why does memory (in the sense we have just been discussing) have independent value?

Perhaps the basic problem with memory – again, only in the sense that we are now discussing – is that it contains exactly the sort of circular connections that get in the way of clear perception and open discussion. It conveys the idea that there is a past that gives meaning to things that we value, and then gets us to believe in the reality of that past because it supports the values that we have. We stand for what we stand for because of the past, and hold a view of the past that conforms to what we stand for. But there is, perhaps, a basic and understandable reason why this obvious failure of logic often gets under the radar – a reason that takes us back to the distinction between personal and collective contexts that this chapter began with.

As persons with family histories, we live in the circle of connections that was just described. We come into existence, most often, in circumstances of unusual intimacy with a small number of people whose views or attitudes or personalities deeply influence the values that we come to form, perhaps by direct teaching, perhaps by a more complicated process that leads us to adapt or react to or reject the lessons that we get. Whether we sign on to or modify or reject the ideas of our earliest models, what we now believe is tied up intimately with our experience of them, and when they leave us, our remembering of them is tied up with reflecting on our own identity. Our memory of them is indeed circular, in that who we are, and what we remember of them, move round and round in what is probably a lifelong way – we cannot finally separate our idea of who we are from early memories. Does anything sufficiently like that take place in a political context, though, or, if it does, are there enough examples of it to sustain a general model of the relationship between a person and his or her political society? Political examples might include intensely politically engaged families in which ideological agreements or disagreements get to be grafted on to parent–child relations, or revolutionary cells that come to function as family surrogates. You may have come to think of Che Guevara as your brother. Outside those special contexts, though, history and belief seem to be very much more weakly related, and to appeal to one in support of the other is very much less clearly compelling.

What truth commissions can do

Truth commissions, of the kind made especially famous by the South African 'Truth and Reconciliation Commission', are among the most notable formal institutions of 'memory' in the modern context. Different examples of the institution have different mandates and powers, but what they have in common is that unlike trials – for which they are often adopted as an alternative – their role is *purely* memorial: that is, they are to create a record, not to convict anyone.[10] As noted above, the creation of a factual record is among their most widely applauded achievements. Trials, of course, also aim to create a factual record in order to support their verdicts, but the facts that can be admitted (and thus recorded) at a trial are limited by the needs of procedural justice, which are strict. Evidence that is prejudicial in certain ways, or inadequately supported, or gathered by inappropriate means, is excluded not because it is deemed to be untrue but in order to safeguard the rights of the accused person. Truth commissions (where no one's rights are on the line) are more open to unchallenged accounts of what victims or witnesses saw.[11] It is possible, then, for a broader and less stringently sifted body of evidence to be assembled, and for general patterns of abuse to emerge from it. And it is also possible, as advocates of truth commissions have pointed out, for victims and witnesses to tell their stories as they see them, without hostile objections or cross-examination. So, without putting a lot of weight on the word 'truth', it becomes possible for another kind of truth to be recorded, 'personal truth' as we may call it, the memories of those who were victimized directly or through the fates of relatives or friends, which are worth recording because of whose memories they are. Together with the discovery of factual truths, this function of truth commissions is widely agreed to have a therapeutic value. And while the therapy can rarely be as simple or instantaneous, surely, as the famous 'revealing is healing' slogan implies, it is clearly among the real benefits of truth commissions for some participants in their work.

But truth commissions also often try to provide another kind of public memory, distinct from either the record of discrete material facts or the narratives of 'personal truth': one that does not fit, either, into the category of 'rehearsal' that was introduced above. Perhaps it would not be misleading to call it 'memory-construction' (MC). Over and above the discovery of facts and the opportunity for personal disclosure, truth commissions that follow the collapse of a regime have the task of building a case against the old regime, a case that confirms the reasons for overthrowing it and thus legitimates its successor. So, given its MC function, a truth commission *is* something like a trial after all – it aims at a verdict that establishes guilt – though with an important difference.

In Chapter 1, we encountered a view about trials that explained their purpose in a particular way. On that view, their purpose is not primarily to deter crime, as is often thought, but to express something about offenders. Offenders have implicitly claimed a sort of privileged status, and their trial and conviction should be seen as dismantling this claim and as reasserting the status of the person whom they victimized. That view makes sense if we think of offences as departures from a norm: The norm says that as citizens we are equal in status, and the offender is guilty of a sort of practical denial of that. His punishment reaffirms the norm. But clearly, this model does not work well in the case of massive, state-sanctioned atrocity, such as a regime in which one group systematically oppresses another, or a military regime directs a 'dirty war' of terror against its opponents. Atrocity of this kind, if not actually made legal, is undertaken by those who legally hold authority. So it is not, as in the case of individual crime, a departure from an established background norm, it is made normal; and those who participate in it – the officials who collect information, the soldiers who obey orders to fire into crowds, the police who arrest and detain without trial, the torturers, the doctors who aid in torture, the lawyers who make a case for torture: the list goes on and on – cannot convincingly be placed in the same category as ordinary criminals. (That is not to say they are better than ordinary criminals; maybe they are worse; but anyway they are different.) So whereas a trial sets out to condemn a person for violating a norm, a truth commission faces the task of condemning a whole set of norms, that is, what the old regime made normal. Hence, MC is a collective, narrative condemnation which resembles a trial of a whole political system rather than of individual offenders.

WHAT MEMORY CALLS FOR

The case for MC is strong, given the need to pass judgement on whole systems. Perhaps the basis for the best case for it was laid by the political philosopher Hannah Arendt, in her book on the trial of Adolf Eichmann, the Nazi war criminal who was kidnapped and put on trial by Israel in 1960.[12] Despite several serious reservations, Arendt finds a morally sustainable case for Eichmann's trial and execution, and in the course of her account, she introduces a powerful idea that she terms 'the banality of evil'. Eichmann was a bureaucrat, whose work resembled the work of other bureaucrats the world over, then as now. He was in charge of providing transportation and other resources that enabled other agencies to do their work. Those agencies were engaged in the work of systematic and brutal extermination. But Eichmann himself never exterminated anyone, nor did he have overall control of the policy of extermination. His work was ordinary or 'banal'. This aspect of Arendt's thinking points forward clearly to the idea of 'the criminal *state*', an idea that invites us to think in terms of condemning whole regimes that turn oppression and cruelty into norms – not necessarily instead of condemning individuals, who can still be held accountable for some of the things that they did, but as well as charging individuals with criminal offences.[13]

So MC has a lot going for it, as a way of constructing large-scale narratives in which the general character of a regime is described and held up for condemnation. How to punish whole regimes is a very hard question,[14] but surely moral accountability – being held up for judgement – is a minimal and acceptable step. And constructing a record of the regime's injustice is an important way to accomplish that. But here are two reservations. Political systems that are familiar to us in the Western world are generally termed 'liberal-democratic', that is to say they embody two kinds of basic political principle; and MC is open to question from the standpoint of both of them – from the standpoint of both liberal and democratic beliefs.

Liberalism, according to the dominant view of it, reflects the belief that a political system ought to guarantee the rights of all its members without officially signing on to views of the world that some of its members reject, thus officially condemning them as wrong. 'Views of the world' obviously embraces many things, but among them would certainly be interpretations of recent history that cast some groups as right and others as wrong, some as (legitimate) winners and others as (deserving) losers. MC, however, does just that. It provides an officially sanctioned narrative that defines some views of the world as those to be approved by society as a whole. Within that narrative, some things, although true, fail the test of what has been called 'aptness'.[15] Let me give a recent Canadian example. At the time of writing, a 'truth and reconciliation' commission is gathering evidence about the Canadian government's effort to assimilate aboriginal people by compelling their children to attend residential schools in which attempts were made to systematically de-culture them. That policy was objectionable in all sorts of ways, both in its conception and its implementation, and the truth and reconciliation commission is clearly charged with demonstrating that. And, to avoid misunderstanding, I think it is right that that should be demonstrated. But the aptness test means that some kinds of evidence are not going to be salient. It is overwhelmingly likely that, as some accounts show, some of the teachers in residential schools were devoted and effective. It has come to light, too, that in some (a small minority of) cases of abuse, the perpetrators of abuse were children rather than teachers. Since this is such a sensitive topic and there is such a risk of misunderstanding, I must repeat that neither of those things mitigates the evil of residential schools in any way, or detracts from the importance of disclosing it. I simply mean that, given the role of the truth and reconciliation commission, certain kinds of evidence are rendered 'inapt', as I think even those who welcome the commission should admit. Maybe a time will come for their aptness, but it is not now.[16]

Very much the same issue comes up in the case of fictional writing about the historical past. Bernhard Schlink asks the following question:

> Even if there might have been a funny moment in Auschwitz, even if there might have been a decent concentration camp guard, even

if there might have been a fairytale element in someone's rescue from persecution and horror – couldn't a novel, a play, a comedy about this make the reader or viewer forget that the full reality was profoundly different?[17]

Of course, in one sense 'the full reality' would include, precisely, all sorts of such atypical details, but what Schlink means is perfectly clear: There are times when looking at the trees prevents us from seeing the wood, and there are times when it is something about the wood that we want people to grasp as vividly as possible, even if some trees have to go unnoticed.

So an institution such as Canada's truth and reconciliation commission is not meant to write a history. It is meant to make a socially important case. It is meant to make a case, moreover, that all Canadian citizens are expected to identify with, and that seems problematic, because Canadians may legitimately hold a range of diverse views about the desirability of assimilation in principle and its success or failure in practice. Is a certain view of the matter something that a liberal state should impose?

Since most Canadian views, as it happens, probably cluster together not too far from the official view, perhaps other cases work better as examples. Traditionally, the white Afrikaner community had its own narrative – a rehearsal memory, as we termed such things – of South African history, a narrative that contained its own epic events and embodied virtues such as god-fearing piety and endurance in the face of (British) oppression. It begins in the eighteenth century, whereas the Truth and Reconciliation Commission's narrative begins in the Apartheid years – it is fairly typical of competing narratives that they begin the story at quite different points that colour later events in very different ways. It would be unusual, and hard to justify given standard liberal principles, to require all South Africans to sign on to a single narrative; not to mention futile. Still more problematic are the cases of Ireland and of Israel–Palestine, where it is surely inconceivable that the two sides should, in the foreseeable future, reach a common account of history; or the case of Lebanon, where the country's own history is such a contentious matter, and so tied up with current political alignments, that the subject is not taught in schools. Of course, in all these cases, the narratives on one side or both can be shown to contain errors of fact and hugely significant omissions. The point is not about the availability of truth, though, it is about whether or not it is reasonable, in a society that accepts and even values difference of opinion, to expect or impose a single story about something so basic as the society's history. A particularly good example is the ongoing contest, among historians and political scientists who study Ireland, between so-called republican and revisionist interpretations of the later twentieth century, 'republicans' emphasizing the role of armed struggle against British rule, 'revisionists' emphasizing, rather, the role of intergovernmental negotiation. The contest is one that policy decisions still find it hard to shake off.[18]

Turning to democracy, it is an attractive idea that after the fall of an oppressive regime a truth commission can be a sort of precursor of democracy, expressing the values of the democratic regime that is to follow.[19] We can easily see how such an idea might arise. Oppressive regimes stifle expression, democratic regimes welcome it, and a truth commission is above all a device that makes expression possible, encouraging and embracing it. It is true that both truth commissions and democracy are unlike oppressive regimes in welcoming expression. But they are not alike in the kind of expression that they need. Once again, what is missing here is the sense in which a truth commission, in its MC aspect, is like a trial in its need to condemn and to reach a verdict. Like all political systems, democracies, too, have to reach decisions, of course, but it is important to the idea of democracy that its decisions are provisional and can be reopened, and that minorities are not proved wrong; they are minorities simply because they do not have the votes right now, not because they are mistaken, and there is no implication that when they are outvoted, they have to change their minds. On some important views of democracy, moreover, public discussion is supposed to be constrained by the desire to win agreement, so that proposals are put forward in ways that could in principle be understood by opponents; as in a conversation, we try to avoid blank confrontation in favour of appeals that invite agreement. But that idea is at odds with the personal-truth aspect of truth commissions, which invites the full disclosure of subjective memory and of the emotions associated with it. They give you your chance to say your piece without inhibition – not to search for common ground.

So – worryingly! – are truth commissions illiberal, in trying to arrive at a common narrative memory, and undemocratic, in trying to arrive at a definitive answer as to what should be remembered? There are two ways to avoid that conclusion. One is to recognize that while truth commissions are not actual examples of liberalism or democracy in operation, they may all the same be valuable prerequisites in the transition from an oppressive regime to a liberal democracy, in that they affirm things that are basic to it. In bringing to light the violence and deceit of the old regime they affirm, by way of contrast, the importance of the values of civility. It cannot be said that they *teach* us those values, for, as Jeremy Waldron has put it,

> the point [of recalling the past] . . . is not that we learn new and better standards for our lives from the judgments we make about the past. Unless we had those standards already, we would not make those judgments.

It is more the case that recalling the past is 'a way of bringing to imaginative life the full implications of principles to which we are already in theory committed'.[20]

On this view, however, there is no very strong connection between us, specifically, and the past of our own society, for other people's examples might do just as well, perhaps even better because more precise and vivid. The ideal moral education – again, on this kind of view – might not be collective memory in the sense of a particular society's recollection and interpretation of its own past, but, rather, a wide-ranging comparative history of many societies' experiences that would be likely to contain a rich supply of examples of different kinds. It would be a cosmopolitan education,[21] not one founded on what is distinctive in a national memory.

That would not of course be nearly enough to satisfy some theorists of memory, who see recollection of *our* past as bound up with who we are. They offer a second view, that all societies (including liberal-democratic ones) need to be 'thickly' connected to their own history so that they can be sustained by a common story; they cannot be liberally neutral or democratically open 'all the way down', as it were. But that idea leads us to a new line of thinking that is reserved for the following chapter.

Public apology

When some past event has been made the subject of public memory, in a way that invites some further response, compensation and apology are the two most apparently available means. Apology seems to follow seamlessly from memory – to recall some unjust event in one's past is at once to feel the need to express regret for it. Or anyway, it should be. And apology is sometimes thought to be the better of the two remedies. In Chapter 2, we noted that, in reaction to unjust enrichment suits, there is the view that suits of that kind commodify slavery, that is, they treat slave labour as an item that could have been bought and sold if only the price were right. Generalizing this point, there is an objection to any kind of financial compensation. Money, one writer objects, 'cannot serve as a proxy for the crimes against humanity and violations of dignity and self-respect inflicted on African slaves', while 'apology brings a sense of humanity and respect to a situation where both humanity and respect had been violated'.[22] Likewise, the very substantial payments made by the (former) German Federal Republic to Israel were resisted, by some Israelis, on the grounds that they implied that a figure could be attached to what the former German regime had done to the Jewish people. It commodified an outrage, they believed, by implying that injustice had a price.[23]

So let us consider the case for (non-commodifying) apology. As in the more general case of memory, the basic model is an individual one, and the collective equivalent is derived from it. There is a pretty standard idea of what an individual apology requires. Here is one account, paraphrased from one of the pioneering discussions of the topic. At least one of the parties involved (the one apologizing and the one being apologized to) must believe that an event took place, and that it was wrong (unjust, offensive); the party making the apology must have been responsible for the event, or connected in some way to whoever was responsible; the party making the apology must regret the event and feel remorse on account of it; and the person receiving the apology must believe that the apologizer intends not to commit the same kind of wrong again.[24] It seems quite true that an attempted apology that failed any of these tests would be defective, and might not even count as (or be received as) an apology at all. (You cannot apologize for something that never happened, that you did not do, that you do not feel at all bad about, and that you openly intend to do in the future.)

Now the fourth condition on this list, which we may call the sincerity condition, is obviously going to be troublesome when we move to the case of public apologies. A personal apology is delivered by a person who is in a certain frame of mind while doing so, and the sincerity condition tells us that the person must be feeling regret and remorse if the apology is to count.[25] Perhaps it is often hard to tell what frame of mind someone is in, but we have standard informal tests (speech inflection, facial expressions) that are often good enough for the purpose. An apology delivered while checking one's email, or while texting a friend about a date, would not do. In any event, there *is* a frame of mind, we know, whether we can reliably detect it or not. A public apology, however, is made by and on behalf of an institution, and it is not at all clear how or to what we can even apply the sincerity test.[26] We are not concerned, presumably, about the sincerity of the spokesperson delivering the apology, or of the person who wrote the text that she is reading from (although we would want the spokesperson to sound sincere, and the scriptwriter to have a convincing way with words). We can assume that in all but the rarest cases, any public statement results from a process to which many people contribute, perhaps, also, for many different reasons. Janna Thompson constructs a hypothetical but very plausible example. She supposes that President Clinton's apology to Guatemala in 1990 for his country's history of political interference emerged from his advisors' view that a new climate was needed in Central-American relations and that there should be a full congressional enquiry into the matter; but other advisors warned against signalling any major policy shift; the outcome was a 'low-key apology' by the President.[27]

So, because public apologies issue from a political process and not from a single mind, and, moreover, are delivered not as any one person's view but as the view of a whole collective, it is quite common to adopt a non-personal definition of sincerity, and to say that in this case, the test of sincerity is the undertaking not to repeat the acts which give rise to the apology, or acts like them.[28] This is a bit awkward, for that undertaking is itself, as we have seen, another of the original criteria for a valid personal apology, and so this proposed solution in effect deletes one of the original criteria. An undertaking not to repeat the injustice covers off and replaces the 'sincerity' concern. That does not seem right, however, given that in actual cases of public apology much is done to convey the *appearance* of sincerity, as though the event was meant to be seen as fully analogous to private apology, and not as being one criterion short. For example, one Canadian attempt at a public apology (for the forced assimilation of aboriginal peoples) was considered a failure because the Prime Minister did not show up at the event, leaving the delivery of the apology to a cabinet minister; and, in another case, the use of the occasion for partisan attacks undermined the apology's effectiveness.[29] Given the obvious importance of apparent sincerity, perhaps the relationship between sincerity and future undertakings ought to be reversed: The future undertaking is not what demonstrates the sincerity, it is the labour-intensive display of sincerity that lends some credibility to promises for the future. If that was not so, there would be no need for, specifically, something with the form of an apology – a promise would do perfectly well instead. A binding constitutional amendment would do even better. The same line of thinking is supported by the view that, rather than (undemonstrable) sincerity, what matters in the case of public apology is that the sentiment expressed should be placed firmly on the public record[30] so that going back on the commitment made or repeating the offence apologized for will be politically embarrassing and perhaps even legally challengeable. The display of sincerity, then, and the apologetic form taken by the process, bear a misleading resemblance to personal apology, for they have an essentially political meaning and function.

The other important way of dealing with the sincerity issue is to make cash payments along with the apology. I do not think many would accept the view that an apology without such compensation is necessarily an empty one, a view that in some intercultural contexts may owe something to translation problems with the word 'apology'.[31] But, other things being equal, a cash payment that accompanies a verbal apology is often taken to reinforce it. This leads to a good deal of confusion, because payments of that kind are often described as 'compensation', as though what we were dealing with here was really an attempt to remedy a loss (or to return a benefit). It is surely better to view it as a token of good faith. As one commentator writes: 'Like the gift I buy for someone I have stood up the payment is a method of putting oneself out, or going out of one's way to apologize.'[32] Words are cheap – free, in fact; and so to accompany them with the sacrifice of an item (money) that is generally taken to be valuable is to show, or try to show, that one means what one says. Blaise Pascal, the great seventeenth-century theologian, said that we express respect for someone by *putting ourselves out* or suffering some inconvenience on his or her behalf – we stand up, for example, to greet someone. (Sitting down or lying down would not work!) In this light, we can arrive at an interpretation of the cheques that accompanied apologies to (e.g.) the Japanese-Americans and Japanese-Canadians who were indiscriminately interned as security risks in the Second World War. There is no plausible way to equate the sums they were given with what they actually lost. But if, added up together, they amount to a not insignificant charge on the governments that paid them, then they may be seen as a demonstration of the donors' seriousness. They have 'put themselves out', in Pascal's words, and that is what counts.

But in the case of more substantial settlements, perhaps there is a different relationship between apology and money. There are many claimants and even more potential claimants to public funds. Governments welcome ways to limit their response. And if claims, to be successful, have to be based on some special case arising from historic injustice, then that implicitly puts an obstacle in the way of claims based simply on need, or on equality. To accompany an apology with money is to demonstrate good faith; to accompany money with an apology is to make the point that distributive justice is not enough, that relief is forthcoming only to the extent that claimants can demonstrate a historical and thus special case for their demands. It is hardly original to point out that the rise of the 'culture of redress', as it is sometimes called, coincided with the decline of the distributive agenda in politics, an agenda sustained by principles of general justice rather than by the facts of historical connection. It is sometimes said that the 'paradigm of distribution', the political world view that underpinned the politics of the left for (roughly) the half-century following the Second World War gave way to the 'paradigm of recognition', a political world view according to which groups' important needs are based on specific historically generated circumstances that states must recognize and respond to.[33] Apology fits squarely within that 'paradigm', and what one makes of it will depend on the larger issue of what one makes of the transition from a class-based to a group-based politics. If you regret the passing (for now? Forever?) of a class-based politics focused on the general redistribution of wealth, you will also regret a political climate in which groups make claims on the basis of their special history. If you believe, though, that it is something other than social class that is the basis of oppression, then you will not shed tears for the passing of the older view of what justice calls for.

But a public apology is not public only in the sense that it is made by a public official, thus giving rise to the sincerity problems discussed above. It is also made in public, and for a public, with the intention of shaping public opinion. This is especially true in cases in which the apology is expressly designed to involve the public in an active way, such as Australia's famous 'national sorry day', a memorial event in which all Australians were encouraged by a report of the Human Rights and Equal Opportunities Commission to recall and regret the many wrongs inflicted on aboriginal inhabitants – it was to be 'a day when all Australians can express their sorrow for the whole tragic episode, and celebrate the beginning of a new understanding . . . as a means of restoring hope to people in despair'.[34] To the extent that publicly sponsored apologies are meant to promote participation in this way, we may see them not as acts of a collective body that speaks for the whole but as attempts to change opinion, so that the apology comes, eventually, to express the aggregated views of the citizens themselves. Then it would not just be an apology by 'Australia' (the state), it would become an apology by 'Australians' (the people: or many of them).

In this section, then, we have identified several things that public apologies can usefully accomplish. First, they can add credibility to an undertaking not to rob or persecute a victim group again, by going through procedures which, whether sincerely meant (by someone) or not, are laborious and thus expressive of a serious commitment, and one that enters the public record in a permanent way. Second, they can be useful items in a political strategy, justified sometimes from some position on the left, sometimes from the right, that disengages government from any general redistributive agenda while enabling it to show that it is not entirely lacking in conscience. Third, they are communicative devices that enable states to convey to their populations that, in case they have not heard yet, it is time for a change of values or attitudes. Those are all things that, depending on one's political point of view, can be valued. They can all help to secure political benefits from one point of view or another. And writers on political apology identify still other benefits not mentioned here.[35] But those benefits, however intensely valued, take us so far away from what is valuable in personal apology that I do not believe there is any real connection at all between the two.

For one could believe passionately in personal apology – be a chronic personal apologizer, apologizing when (for example) one's tennis opponent could not return one's serve – without signing on to any of the purposes of political apology; and conversely, one could advocate any of these purposes of political apology while being utterly churlish about apologies in real life. There is an ethical imperative behind personal apologies. It reflects the basic human fact that we all fall short of our ideals, and need to express regret when we do, and the other basic human fact that in realizing our own ideals, we often tragically disappoint the ideals of others. That makes personal apology basic to the human condition itself. But we cannot get from there to political apology, which, to the extent that it is justifiable, rests on different justifications altogether. And one cannot get to those justifications by way of valuing apology itself – any more than one can get to memorial events by way of valuing memory itself. Those personal obligations that we have, by virtue of memory and apology, do not translate into public obligations, and public obligations cannot be justified in the same basically compelling way.

From apology to identity

But, as noted above, and as you will know if you have read any of the works on memory and apology mentioned in the Notes to this chapter, at least one important line of argument has not even been considered here. This is the line of argument that concerns *identity*. It tells us that to take steps to remember, or to apologize, is to say something about – or in some cases to change – the way in which we identify the nature of ourselves or of our society. Both memory and apology do so either because they acknowledge things that we have tried to ignore or suppress, or else because they express a determination to revise the values that have defined our practices in the past. (And once again, there is some transfer here of models familiar in the personal context to social or political use.) I have not ignored these arguments because I think they are unimportant. On the contrary, I have bracketed them here because they are much too important to be treated as a subtheme in a chapter such as this, and so they will now get a chapter to themselves. How is redress connected to identity, and which of our 'identities' provides the most compelling basis for historical redress?

4
BECAUSE WE ARE WHO WE ARE

Some arguments for redress, as we noted in the previous chapter, are based on *identity*. They do not (basically) invoke the rights of those who suffered in the past, or the present benefits that can be traced to their suffering, or the necessity of remembering suffering: They simply ask us to think about who we are. Here is one version of the view: We are in history, and history does not consist of a series of unrelated facts but of sequences that may continue for many centuries.[1] Some very ancient sequences have run their course, but others, including most or all of those that give rise to claims for redress, are not yet over. When historians of the future write about our present, they would not draw a sharp line between our present and the two world wars, between our present and colonialism, between our present and the dispossession of aboriginal peoples, because the stories that those events began have not ended yet. We can still do things that will change the way those stories will be written, as we cannot in the case of (let us say) the stories in the Old Testament. (We can now do nothing for Job.) So there is a sense in which we are still *in* the history of the Second World War, or of imperialism, and we wrongly deny that if we take the view that we have no responsibility for what was done in the earlier stages of that history. As British or American people we cannot dissociate ourselves from the bombing of the German city of Dresden in 1944, because historians of the future will want to know what we eventually made of it: Did we decide that it was justified, modifying the rules of war to permit the destruction of civilian targets, or did we respond by regretting it and by taking steps to uphold the protection of civilians in the present and future? No doubt everyone in the world should think about that – it is important for the world as a whole to understand the rules of war – but it is as citizens of the nations whose air forces conducted the bombing raids that we have to think about it, because it is those nations that are connected to it by their history.

Here is another version. Political theorists often like to think of political systems in very abstract ways; they fall into the category of 'democracy', for example, or they express certain ideas of 'justice'. But those kinds of abstractions are not actually what bind a society together and enable it to have a political life.[2] Societies are bound together by much more specific sorts of ideas or images or models or heroes. In the case of the United States, for example, the personality and rhetorical brilliance (and fate) of Martin Luther King are certainly more influential than the abstract idea of equality that academics discuss. Another reference point is the integration of black athletes (previously segregated) into professional baseball leagues in the United States in the 1960s. Sport is hugely important: In the Canadian case, it was true for many years – though memories are fading now – that a marker of identity was caring about 'the Henderson goal', a desperate last-minute goal that won Canada a hockey victory over Russia in 1972. Nowadays, it is probably the public provision of health care that is taken as a marker of Canadianness (as opposed to Americanness). In the case of countries with longer histories, such as Britain, there are so many events from Magna Carta to the Battle of Agincourt to 1688 to Munich and Dunkirk and the Miners' Strike and the Falklands War that I hardly know how to draw up a list. Politics, as some view it, is basically a matter of the *interpretation* of such symbolically charged events, events that have local meaning, not of the analysis of abstract concepts. So when we respond to some significant past event, we are helping to define who we are. This has a particular importance, of course, for past injustices committed by our society. A people who does not care about some past injustice is different in character from a people who acknowledges its wrongness. For this reason, the acknowledgement of past injustice, coupled with apology and compensation when that is appropriate, is an important way for a society to interpret and define its own political character. It is to say who we take ourselves to be, and that ought to change how we behave in the here-and-now and in the future.

Those are not the only two versions of the view that this chapter considers. Later in the chapter, a third will be introduced, one that raises somewhat different questions. But those two are certainly enough to be going on with for now. Do we have to do things about the past because of who we are? And do those two views give us a definite enough idea of who we are and what follows from that?

Relationship terms

To the first question – do we have to do things because of who we are? – the answer has to be 'yes', and to the second, 'yes, but . . .'

The first answer has to be 'yes' because the appeal to 'who I am' or 'who you are' is among the most common ways of justifying or criticizing behaviour.[3] In the ordinary course of things, we rarely if ever appeal to some large moral theory. Quite often, we may appeal to some general rule-of-thumb, such as 'do unto others . . .' or some parable (such as the Good Samaritan story) of general importance. But at least as often, perhaps more, we go straight to statements of identity. If someone asks you why you are buying a birthday present for your daughter, 'Because she is my daughter' is as good and complete an answer as one could give. (Well, we could of course construct special cases in which your daughter has been horrid to you, and a friend is expressing surprise at your generosity – but let us stick to standard cases.) And if you object to someone's lying to a friend of theirs, 'Because he is your friend' is really all you need to say to explain your objection. The simple fact of being daughters or friends, sons or

BECAUSE WE ARE WHO WE ARE

spouses or brothers, is enough to convey that there are rights and wrongs as to how they should be treated. Some people think that this is because, just below the surface, we are actually appealing to an unstated general rule, such as 'friends should be helped', a rule so obvious that we need not usually spell it out.[4] But in reply to this, it has been pointed out that we do not need the rule, all we need to have is an understanding of what 'friend' means. If you do not have that, then you do not know how to use the word, and if you do have it then you do not need the rule.[5] Not only that, but even if we did imagine a rule book for friends, or brothers, it would not give us right or wrong answers about how to behave to *this* friend or *this* brother, because we are related to particular friends or particular brothers in particular ways; they depend on us in particular ways, they have helped us in particular ways, and the right or wrong thing to do will be coloured by sharing with them a history that other friends and other brothers do not have.

So far, so good. The stage may seem to be nicely set for moving on to 'I am a Canadian' and taking 'Canadian' to mean being part of a society with a particular history that gives rise to particular kinds of claims and debts – for which redress must then be made. But before we get there, two problems have to be faced and if possible overcome. We may call them problems that concern the 'strength' and the 'scope' of the idea.

'Strength' first. It is certainly true that relationship terms are very powerful, leading us immediately to a whole set of responses about what is right and wrong. And it is also certainly true that we arrive at these responses without consulting a sort of mental rule-book about relationships – let alone without consulting Kant or other great moral theorists. But it is no less certainly true that the responses that we have to relationship matters are sometimes questioned, and should be. It was once taken for granted, for example, that in societies based on the hereditary principle those who had wealth and power should be able to pass them on to their children (sons, or eldest sons). It was once taken for granted, more recently than that, that men could force sexual relations on their wives. In India, until the nineteenth century, many took it for granted that it was a widow's duty to throw herself onto her husband's funeral pyre. And no doubt people who favoured such things would have justified them in terms of the 'meaning' of terms such as 'son', 'wife', 'widow'. So I do not think we should feel comfortable about the general idea of justifying practices on the basis of what relationship words 'mean'. To be sure, it is safe enough to assume that feelings about what relationships mean spring from the relationship itself, not from any large moral theory. But if we give immediate recognition to duties attached to relationships, that can only be because we regard them as consistent with broader ideas of right and wrong, and experience no awkward inner dissonance. We can give birthday presents, but not political power, to our sons; and we can explain it by saying, simply, 'well, he's my son'; but that is an explanation only because ideas about what should happen between parents and children have been sifted and modified, over the years, by ideas about social justice, ideas that put gifts of tricycles on one side of a line and gifts of political power on the other. So the apparent strength of appeals to 'who we are' may be a bit misleading, if they are as strong as they are exactly because they have been lent strength by virtue of being endorsed by something more general in its ethical reach.

It used to be thought, before the rise of modern ideas of the state and of law, that families inherited grievances that their members had a duty to avenge. (See, e.g. *Romeo and Juliet*.) Over generations, extended families essentially waged war against each other for the sake of honour, and it is pretty well a certainty that at many points in the history of the vendetta, the explanation 'Because you're a . . . [e.g. Capulet]' was used to convey the duty of vengeance to young male family members. Modern legal and political systems are built around quite different ways of settling grievances, and where vendettas survive, they are regarded as unfortunate relics of more violent times. I think that should give us pause when we are told, for example, that we are so bound up with our society that our identity tells us 'for what

BECAUSE WE ARE WHO WE ARE

crimes we must make amends'.[6] Exactly the same line of thinking – your place in history places moral burdens on you – could just as well tell us 'for what crimes we must exact revenge from others'. The important point that this demonstrates is that we have to think critically when we are told that because we are so-and-so we have to do such-and-such. (Isn't that the moral of *Romeo and Juliet*?)

Secondly, 'scope'. Examples of close personal relationships were used above to make the point that we are considering – child, spouse, friend and so on. They are the best examples, but it would not be right to think that the point concerns only relationships of that kind. For example, professional roles are also thought to give rise to similarly immediate responses. Think of 'Stand back please, I'm a doctor'. Professional relationships, like family ones, give rise to special rights and wrongs, ones that do not apply across the board. There are things that doctors, lawyers, police officers, teachers can do that others cannot do, and things that they cannot do that others can do, because they are doctors, lawyers, police officers, teachers. This sort of case is a bit less clear than the family case, because for obvious enough reasons the rights and wrongs of professionals are written down and enforced – 'professional ethics', they are called. But perhaps we can suppose that, as is sometimes claimed, the written-down and enforced versions are just ways of making explicit what the role itself requires. That psychiatrists are forbidden to sleep with their patients, for example, is not just some puritanical rule imposed, from the outside, on the practice of psychiatry, but something necessary to the patient's trust that enables effective therapy to be carried out, and, therefore, for the patient–doctor relationship to make sense.

So let us not just suppose that 'Because I'm an x' is the sort of explanation that is confined to very personal settings. There are wider settings where it makes sense, if slightly less direct sense. But do those wider settings include the nation-state, as they will have to do if our 'identity' is taken to include responsibility for what our nation-states have done?

Nation, or state?

To discuss that question, the very first thing we have to do is take apart the idea of the 'nation-state', in order to get at the basic arguments for redress. We have to have some general term, of course, to refer to the entities among which the world is divided, and 'nation-state' conveniently covers the fact, sort of, that those entities are both social or cultural things (nations) and political and legal things (states). But there are very few nation-states, if those are taken to be nations combined with states in something close to a one-to-one way. (Japan? Iceland?) Almost all states embrace many nations, and some nations have no states. Some straddle state boundaries. Setting even that aside, the ideas of 'nation' and 'state', even in cases where they do overlap, are quite different, and lead us in the direction of quite different ways of accounting for what, it is held, we are called on to do.

Whole books have been written about what 'nation' and 'state' mean, but let us go straight to what the distinction has to do with redress. According to some views, redress is due because wrong was done by co-*nationals* of ours, related to us by traditions or values or a culture that we share with them.[7] According to other views, redress is due because wrong was done by co-*citizens* of ours, related to us by a system of political and legal authority.[8] Very interestingly, each of these views claims that it can do something important that the other cannot do, that is, establish continuity with the past. According to the nation-based view, nations have historical continuity while states do not, because political systems change radically while nations retain their underlying character. According to the state-based view, however, nations are made up of successive generations, while states are continuous things, institutions that are recognized as legally abiding entities with obligations that survive generational change. This is an important matter for the issue of redress, because it does not just affect which body we are to attach any duties of redress to, it also affects the basic reasons that we should hold for believing that redress is due to anyone at all. Do we owe it because we are connected to the original wrongdoers by values or culture, or because we have citizenship in a state that committed (or approved, or tolerated) the original wrongdoing?

It may seem natural to think of nations as things that endure longer than states. It is not that they do not undergo change, perhaps eventually becoming transformed, but it is natural to think that they change more slowly, being made up of attitudes and beliefs and customs that are less easy to modify than political or legal institutions. But as a corrective let us look at two contrasting real-world examples, one North American and one European, from the later twentieth century. The North American example: In the mid-twentieth century, the Canadian province of Quebec (which calls itself a 'nation' within the Canadian federation) began a process known as the 'Quiet Revolution'. From the beginning of Canadian history, Quebec had been economically backward, colonized by outsiders, dominated by the Catholic church, and deeply conservative in its social attitudes. Within a decade or so, it transformed itself in all of these respects, and apart from the fact that it remained a predominantly French-speaking society, all the markers of its identity changed.

The European example: At around the same time, France had transformed its political identity, dissolving the 'Fourth Republic' and becoming the 'Fifth Republic' by virtue of adopting a new constitution that differed from the previous one mainly in enhancing the executive branch by providing for a directly elected president. There continued to be a national legislature, elected in the same way as before; and the legal system and the rights of citizens remained unchanged. No one supposed that its public debt was cancelled or that its treaty obligations were nullified or that citizens had to reapply for membership or that the national anthem had to be rewritten.

Quebec, then, radically changed its culture and values while remaining the same 'nation'; France modified its political system in significant but marginal ways and became a new 'republic'. I think this ought to warn us against thinking that nations are somehow more abidingly stable things than states are. We call nations the same even when they transform themselves radically, while calling states different when they modify their political arrangements somewhat. It is hard to see how it can be a general truth that nations, defined in terms of values or culture, can be more enduring things than states, when national values and culture may change, and when states may change in less drastic ways even when they are called by a different name. In both cases, we may well see reasons to doubt whether it is quite clear that identity has or has not changed. It seems to depend. If language is more important to you than religion, you will say that Quebec stayed the same, despite the Quiet Revolution, because Quebec remained French speaking. If you are a passionate believer in parliamentary democracy, you will say that France became a different place when a presidential system was adopted. We touch here on a very old question in the history of philosophy. How much change and what kind of change can a thing undergo without becoming a different thing? When every part of a ship is replaced piece-by-piece, to use the traditional example, is it still the same ship?

That objection would seem to apply in an even-handed way, leading to scepticism about both nation-based and state-based views. Perhaps we really do not have very definite ideas about when to say that something is the same or that it is different. Isn't that famous ship simply the same in one sense (structure) and different in another (materials)? But the issue does not rest wholly on questions about what identity is. There is another consideration that tells against the nation-based view, even if we set aside examples of surprisingly rapid national change. According to that view, responsibility flows from signing on to a set of broadly shared values. If I value 'Englishness', I am responsible for what England has done or is doing. If I value 'Germanness', I am responsible for what Germany has done or is doing.

We could certainly raise critical doubts about whether Englishness or Germanness actually exist in a very coherent way and if so whether there is just one idea of either of them, but even taking the view on its own terms, there is a problem about the relationship between values, on the one hand, and what is actually *done*, on the other. No doubt it is true that all actions except random ones can be traced back to something that is valued by the person who is acting. But how people get from values to action is a complicated and variable matter, and people declaring loyalty to the same values can reach different and in fact violently opposite conclusions about what to do. Likewise, people holding very different values can arrive at very similar conclusions about what to do – (some) Catholics may arrive at views about abortion that are much closer to those of (some) Muslims than they are to the views of (some) non-Catholic Christians (or even some Catholics). That makes the same point from the opposite angle: Where people start, in terms of values, may not always say much about where they end up, in terms of politics. They can start at the same place in terms of values and end up with different politics, or start with different values and end up with the same politics. So to hold people responsible for where other people with the same values have ended up does not seem right. Let us briefly consider three examples: one of Englishness, one of Germanness and one of Americanness.[9]

In 1944, the Bishop of Chichester, George Bell – who as a Bishop in the Church of England had a seat in the House of Lords – spoke out forcefully against the saturation-bombing of German cities (such as Dresden) by the air forces of his country and the United States. His argument was that the end sought – unconditional surrender by Germany, allowing the Allies to dictate terms of peace – did not justify the enormous loss of civilian lives caused by the firestorms that the bombing produced. Bishop Bell was undoubtedly a patriot, who regretted that his country's name and official faith were shamefully blackened by indiscriminate violence, and who appealed to notions of justice and fairness that he had reason to believe his compatriots would and should respect. Those who supported saturation-bombing, however, maintained both that patriotic opinion in Britain demanded repayment in kind for the German bombing of British cities, and that the threat posed by Naziism to the British way of life was so profound that no negotiated peace was thinkable, even if the death toll was greatly increased.

In the same year – in an episode later dramatized in the movie *Valkyrie* – a group of very senior German officers conspired unsuccessfully to end the war by assassinating Hitler. They too were certainly patriots, members of an officer class likely to regard Hitler and his crew as ill-bred upstarts, and holding a view of national interest that led them to fear total defeat, especially at the hands of Russian invaders and occupiers. They were horribly punished for their treachery, and one can hardly deny that the Nazi regime that executed them was itself sustained by an idea, however perverted, of Germanness, an idea drawing upon stylized and mythic interpretations of German culture and history.

Shortly after the end of the Second World War, politics in the United States was derailed by the 'McCarthyism' epidemic. Senator Joe McCarthy hunted down people with liberal views, many of whom had had connections of varied degrees of seriousness with the Communist Party, using the rhetorically powerful charge that they were 'un-American'. That was of course to seize the high ground, for being 'un-American' in the context of US politics at the time was to lose any claim to enjoy legitimacy. The beginning of the end for Senator McCarthy, however, was when he tried to extend the reach of his smear campaign to the Army, enabling President (formerly General) Eisenhower to make a politically devastating broadcast in which he branded McCarthy as unpatriotic for attacking a major national institution.

In all three cases, what it *means* to be 'patriotic' – to be truly British, German, American – is exactly what is contested. Bishop Bell and Prime Minister Churchill, General von Stauffenberg and Adolf Hitler, Senator McCarthy and President Eisenhower, all claimed the mantle of patriotism, but clashed with each other in terms of the right thing to do. If this point sometimes gets obscured, I think that is because of rather ill-thought-out ideas about ends and means. 'Ends' are in some sense more important than means, because unless we know what ends we are trying to achieve, it hardly makes sense to spend time thinking about the 'means' that could bring them about. After all, why think about how to get something if you do not want or value it? But it does not follow that there is a sort of two-step process whereby we first settle on ends and then start thinking about means, as though decisions about ends were now over and done with. There is a feedback loop. When we think about what means will cost, we have to go back to our proposed ends in order to see if they justify the cost. If they do not, they are not ends that we should adopt. Rather than thinking in a dualistic way about ends and means, it would be better, then, to think in terms of choosing between sets of ends-and-means together – whole political programmes, in other words, with their objectives and their implementation both spelled out.

If that is so, we can certainly be held responsible for giving some support to a whole programme of ends-plus-means. But for giving support to some 'ends' that also figure in some other programme that is quite different from a practical point of view? That seems very dubious. I do not see why, because I identify myself as British, or German, or American, I should be held responsible for things that others do on the basis of interpretations of Britishness, Germanness or Americanness that I find to be bizarre or even perhaps entirely incomprehensible or perverted, and which – in terms of *my* interpretation of the national values in question – I would find alien.

It is sometimes argued, however, that if you are part of something you can be held to account for if it goes bad; if, for example, you are part of an initially peaceful demonstration that leads to property damage, or if you are one of a group of joy-riding youths (not the driver) that runs someone down.[10] It seems to me that we have to know quite a bit more before we hold people accountable for what others in their group have done. If the demonstration, though non-violent, was predictably inflammatory, for example, we might hold all of its members responsible, but not if some people among the demonstrators were exploiting a peaceful protest as a cover for provocation. If the joyriders were driving recklessly on a city street, it would be one thing and something else if they were driving around a normally deserted field. Judgements may differ, but at least it would seem we have to *make* a judgement, and it will be about how closely an individual person's intention was related to the outcome. Their connection to what happened would not be automatic. We might also want to distinguish between a person's feeling bad about his or her participation in something and outsiders' blaming him or her for it. As a well-behaved partygoer at a party that gets so out of hand that even tolerant neighbours call the police, one might feel ashamed or embarrassed, even want to apologize to the neighbours despite being personally blameless, but it would be a different matter if everyone at the party were to be punished in some way, just for being there.

The point becomes clearer if we contrast the idea of national responsibility with the enormously important idea of taking responsibility for one's own, personal, past. In a chapter devoted to that, a book on *The Moral Demands of Memory* makes effective use of two cases, one fictional, the other real.[11] The fictional case is that of the title character in the novel (and movie) *Felicias's Journey*, about an Irish girl who naively seeks out the entirely unreliable father of her child, falls in with a man who persuades her to have an abortion, who tries to take advantage of her, tries to kill her when he fails and then commits suicide. The real-world case is that of George Wallace, the brutally segregationist governor of Alabama, who, after being paralysed in an assassination attempt, became a prominent spokesman for civil rights. In both cases, the author (ethicist Jeffrey Blustein) argues, we can see the importance to individuals of recollecting their pasts and actively making an assessment of it. Felicia comes to see that she herself (among others, of course) was an agent in her own past. Wallace comes to see that his change of heart demands that he actively make amends by political action. Blustein offers a very insightful three-part account of what is meant by taking responsibility for what was done: reconstructing the meaning of the past from the present standpoint, appropriating it or recognizing it as one's own and 'thematizing' it or deriving from it some recurrent themes or motifs that one sees as (good or bad) features of oneself with which one must come to terms. There is a good fit between this and the typical aims of psychotherapy (which, as Blustein notes, speaks rather in favour of that technique as opposed to the use of psychotropic drugs, which short-circuits valuable reflective processes). But that surely makes the point that what is of value here is a sort of personal integration, a coming together as a person, that is only distantly related to national identification. We should not expect the relation between you and something else to be as close as the relation between different parts or phases of you. If one has personally supported some act of one's nation, then that amounts to an act in one's own past that one must come to terms with, just as one must come to terms with what one has done in one's private life. If you were a vocal advocate of 'harsh interrogation methods' (more generally called torture), then you must come to terms with what happened to Iraqi prisoners at Abu Ghraib. That you are simply proud of being an American does not carry that responsibility, if, as I have argued, being American (or British or German) can mean many different things, and can be meant differently by different people.

The South African novelist J. M. Coetzee might disagree. Responding to news of the atrocious treatment of prisoners in Iraq, his first-person character in *Diary of a Bad Year* says: 'If today I heard that some American had committed suicide rather than live in disgrace, I would fully understand.'[12] Only a bit less uncompromisingly, others argue that one is on the hook for what one's country does unless one has strenuously and publicly opposed it.[13] That too seems overly demanding, although it may depend on the costs and difficulty of opposition. If opposition is easy then yes, failing to oppose is the sort of omission that counts as an action, and so you can be held accountable just as you can be held accountable for active support of something. If opposition is costly, then we do not normally hold people morally accountable for failing to be saints or heroes. (We applaud saints and heroes, after all, just because they do much more than they have to.)

Complicity

If we are looking for ways to hold people accountable for what is done in their name, perhaps states give us a better basis than nations do. Nations are amorphous things, defined by values or traditions that need constant interpretation, and whose meanings are frequently contested, even if we concede that there is some sense in which they have a single set of values or beliefs. (Cases of deeply divided nations, or nations with very distinct minorities within them, would naturally make things even trickier than in the simpler case.) States, on the other hand, are organizations with a defined structure, with definite responsibilities, and (unlike nations) they actually make decisions; moreover, and this is what I most want to stress, they rest on consent. People do not of course choose the state that they are born in any more than they choose the nation that they are born in, but states exist because people support them, in however minimal a way, by their actions. They pay taxes to their states, sometimes fight to defend their states, and by their compliance with the states' demands make possible the powers at their disposal. This is of course risky: To lend one's support to a power that one does not control is to take a leap in the dark; and among the risks that arise is that one's state will use its power unjustly against outsiders or against minorities within – thus doing things that will later give rise to claims to redress.

Because of this, it seems much more plausible to hold people accountable as members of states than as members of nations. When some injustice is done in the name of the nation that you belong to, whether or not you support the injustice is an open question, given that what a particular nation is or stands for is such an open-ended matter. What 'Americanness' is said to demand may have nothing do with – may fly in the face of – Americanness as you understand it. You can honestly dissociate yourself from it. But you cannot in the same way dissociate yourself from actions that have been made possible, in however small a way, by your own support.

Of course, the kind and degree of support will vary hugely, both because individual roles vary so much and because political systems vary greatly in the kind of 'consent' that they rely on. The accountability of people must be graded according to the kind of support they have given, and the murderous thugs who carry out leaders' orders bear more responsibility than tax-paying bystanders. In some political systems, there are significant opportunities for citizens to give or withdraw consent, while in others consent takes the form of acquiescence. Where acquiescence is the result of state terror, so that the cost of refusing support is lethal, I think most people would want to say that it does not give rise to any responsibility at all, amounting to 'consent' only in a hopelessly stretched sense of the term. The seventeenth-century political philosopher Thomas Hobbes maintained that consent given at gunpoint was just as binding as any other kind. After all (to paraphrase his view), you are offered a choice between giving up your money or your life, and you choose to give up your money – just as, when offered a choice between seeing a movie and going roller-skating, you choose (say) roller-skating. But someone who offers you a choice between giving up your money or your life is making you an instrument of his will, as someone who offers you a choice between seeing a movie and going roller-skating is not. And the tyrant is like the gunman, not like someone who is trying to find out what your entertainment preferences are. Despite Hobbes's argument, your will is – effectively – no longer your own, and responsibility does not follow from your 'choice' not to oppose a tyrant.

Ruling out cases where compliance is the result of state terror, then, we have at least the beginning of an argument for holding people accountable for things that they did not do, but which – perhaps, again, in only a small way – they made possible. Accountability reaches them not as members of a nation, supposedly committed to some common value, but as citizens of states, organizations that can act because of their members' compliance. For this reason, we may lean towards theories of redress that pin duties of redress on states rather than nations, not because we can settle the question of whether states or nations are more continuous in time – or the classic question of whether a totally reconstructed ship is still the same ship! – but because it makes more sense for the costs of redress to fall on people as members of states. They have, in a small way, *done* something.

While this may give us the beginning of an argument, it is pretty clear that it is no more than that. As it stands, it will pin responsibility on only one generation, that is, the generation of adult citizens who complied – and then only in cases in which non-compliance was not a lethal choice – with a state that was committing injustice. But responsibility for historical redress, as we have defined it, must cross generations, and so we need a further argument if we are to show that it can fall not only to a generation that contributed indirectly but to later generations that cannot be said to have contributed at all, indirectly or otherwise. They did not *do* anything, after all, they were not even there.

Political continuity

Here we turn to the third identity-based approach, mentioned above. It should get a section to itself, not only because it comes at a crucial point in the development of this book's argument, but also because it is by far the most carefully worked-out approach so far to the issue of historical redress. It is the view that, as a member of a politically organized society, one is necessarily part of a system of commitments that span generations. You may not have done anything, but because of who you are, you cannot close your eyes to what your politically organized society has done. Before moving on, let us signal a shift of terminology here. What was referred to above as a 'state', and what was just called a 'politically organized society', is referred to by Janna Thompson, the philosopher who has developed the view that we are about to consider, as a 'polity' – 'a political society that persists through time and across generations: an organized entity capable of acting as an agent and taking responsibility for its actions'.[14]

This view, too, arises from the judgement that a political identity is better fitted than national identity as the starting-point for an argument for redress. To be sure, we may concede, strong claims can be made about the kind of feelings that people develop with their nations, feelings that lead them to identify with both their past triumphs and their past mistakes; but not everyone has such feelings, nor does everyone feel that his or her personal life story is so tightly bound up with the history of his or her nation that it makes no sense without it. Similarly, strong claims are made, though perhaps less commonly, about the value of political society, which can also be seen as a sort of arena in which people can act in ways that give meaning to their lives.[15] But we hardly need anything like that to get the idea going. All we need is the idea that people have interests in things that extend beyond their own lives, something already discussed in Chapter 1. They may want to leave a good reputation behind them. They may want to transmit property to children, or to charitable causes. They may want a business or farm to flourish as a result of their work. They may want to pass on a culture, or political beliefs. They may wish not to be the last generation on earth, a terrifying prospect described by P. D. James in her novel, *The Children of Men*, terrifying because of the sense of pervasive futility that it would lead to. James's novel brings out brilliantly the way in which what we think of as a human life is inherently bound up with intergenerational continuity.

This affects the polity in two related ways. First, it means that in some important ways, it must provide the conditions under which people can reasonably hope to promote intergenerational interests; for example, it has to provide legal mechanisms by which property can be transferred from one generation to another.[16] That of course means that the polity itself must survive over generations, or it could not provide those conditions. Second, though, the polity itself needs to make commitments, on its own account, that stretch beyond one generation. It needs to make binding treaties with other polities in order to promote its interests and security. It needs to raise money, borrowed against future revenue. And it would be hopelessly constrained, in doing what it is meant to do, if it could not make decisions that affect future generations one way or another. Because of this, each generation inherits a set of opportunities and limits from the past, and in turn transmits another set of opportunities and limits to the future.

While that tells us something about the forward-looking responsibilities of a polity, does it tell us enough about why it inherits debts that it is bound to settle? The answer that is offered is that in acting on the principle that each political generation can pass on commitments to the future, it implicitly binds itself to carrying out the commitments that it has inherited. Or, in place of the term 'principle', we could adopt the term 'moral practice' that we used earlier, in Chapter 1, in talking about inheritance and deathbed promises. As members of a polity, we are engaged in a moral practice of intergenerational binding, and it would be morally inconsistent to think that we could adopt part of that practice – the part that allows us to bind the future – while rejecting another part – that part that allows the past to bind us. We must treat like cases alike, and the past- and future-related cases *are* alike.

Now we do as a matter of fact bind the future quite extensively: but some argue that we should not do so. Fiscal conservatives, for example, take the view that it is wrong to pass on a public debt to future generations, on the grounds that it is unjust to make others pay our expenses, and inefficient for us not to face the full cost of our decisions. If we reply that certain projects would become unaffordable if the cost could not be spread between generations, then we run into moral relativists who tell us that we have no reason to think future generations will think those projects are valuable just because we find them to be. (Who knows if future generations will appreciate the intergenerationally financed space programme, for example?) And if we reply, to that, that some things are not based on preference but demanded by justice, then we confront radical democrats who say that it is not enough that policies be just, they have to be chosen by each generation, which has self-determining powers. Thomas Jefferson is famous for his view that, in a democracy, one generation should not even impose a permanent constitution on future generations, each generation being free to rewrite it. Every 19 years, he argued, given the voting age and life expectancy in his time, there is in effect a new majority among the electorate, and unless they can express their acceptance or rejection of constitutional arrangements, they are being ruled, illegitimately, by the dead hand of the past.[17]

These objections may somewhat limit the scope of the idea that we are considering, but they may not defeat it. Perhaps public debt *should* be stringently limited, for various reasons, among them the concern about respecting future generations' freedom to make their own judgements of priority; but of course, that reason reasserts the principle that we have responsibilities to the future, it just interprets it in a particular way, one that stresses preserving fiscal freedom rather than the provision of public goods. We can concede something to the moral relativists while still insisting that our successors, although different, will still be, like us, mortal air-breathing mammals, and that we can predict quite a range of their just needs without knowing very much about their perhaps special world view. As for the radical democrats, the view is self-defeating. It requires us to adopt constitutional provisions that will prevent the next generation from unjustly binding the generation after that, and that will of course mean than we are taking one very important decision out of the next generation's hands.[18]

So the idea that we are considering seems basically good: Even if people interpret it restrictively, there *is* an intergenerational moral principle or practice that means we should take inherited duties seriously, as the counterpart of doing things that commit future generations. But there are still some questions about what this means for the idea of historical redress.

The clearest case for the idea is that of a treaty – an international treaty, or a treaty made by a colonial power with native peoples. Treaties are pointless if they expire when their signers do. Their whole point is that they bind – well, maybe not forever, but for an indefinite period, until circumstances have so changed that the terms of the original agreement are plainly obsolete from the point of view of both parties. In the settler societies of North America and New Zealand, many claims for redress arise from treaty obligations, and it is here that the view we are considering is in its natural element. Polities that still exist today have unmet treaty obligations to native societies that still exist today, and the case for meeting those obligations is no different from the case for keeping a promise. Difficulties arise, of course, in connection with the means of meeting them, for the physical environment has been transformed since the eighteenth century, and immigrant newcomers from the nineteenth and twentieth centuries have claims upon much of it; but that is only a reason to renegotiate what is owed, not to cancel it.[19]

But the idea that we are considering is not meant to be limited to cases covered by treaty obligations. It is meant to justify redress in the case of all kinds of injustices committed in the past – including, importantly, the case of Australia, where no treaties with aboriginals were made, the colonial power embracing the useful fiction that the land was empty; and here it becomes much less clear that the idea works. We can say that, in addition to acquiring special kinds of obligation by making treaties, polities have a general obligation to look after the basic interests of their members and those who fall under their care, and that when they fail to look after them, or, worse, actually damage them, they need to make redress for having done so. They certainly do have an obligation of care. A problem, though, is that they have failed in it so often that the list of possible claimants is very long. In the case of failing to meet a treaty obligation, we know exactly who it is that has a claim, that is, the other party to the treaty. In the case of failing in a general responsibility to look after people's interests, we confront quite a list. Women, whose political rights and rights to physical security were denied; children, denied education and compelled to work in mines, factories and chimneys; industrial workers, denied protection against industrial accidents; religious minorities, denied freedom of worship; sexual minorities, denied recognition; soldiers and sailors, treated as expendable cannon fodder. Once we get beyond the limited range of treaty-based claims, then, there seems to be no ready way to pick

BECAUSE WE ARE WHO WE ARE

out deserving claimants among all those who suffered at the hands of, or with the permission of, the states of the eighteenth, nineteenth and twentieth centuries, whose failures of responsibility were almost universally appalling.

As the Introduction noted, in some cases, the victims of state abuse or neglect are still identifiable as groups – unlike the descendants of sailors in eighteenth-century warships, or the victims of nineteenth-century industrial accidents. Where victim groups are still identifiable, the Introduction also noted, there is a cynical explanation for the attention that they get – there is political capital to be made out of their history. But there is a non-cynical reason too. They still exist, as identifiable groups, because what happened to aboriginal people or African slaves in the eighteenth century still affects their descendants today. That they still exist as identifiable groups is itself evidence of this. That there aren't enclaves of the descendants of eighteenth-century sailors, nursing their rum ration and cursing Lord Nelson, is evidence that the wrong done to them has now been dissipated. Some wrongs endure, however, in an embodied way, that is, in the bodies and minds of those who still suffer them despite distance in time from the original wrong.

That gives us an answer to the question that was posed in the last paragraph but one. No doubt the misdeeds and omissions of eighteenth-, nineteenth- and twentieth-century states give rise to an unmanageable list, but in some cases – that is, cases in which the original wrong is still experienced – we have a reason for special concern. But that answer comes at a price, for the argument in question. If 'what is owed depends on present needs', and historic obligations survive 'as long, and only as long, as history is relevant to the interests of present and future citizens',[20] then what we face is a case of *present* injustice; and while it demands our attention, so do many other cases. That there are people among us who suffer deprivation because of what the previous managers of our polity did is undeniably important. That there are refugees among us because of the hideous cruelty of the current managers of other polities is also undeniably important. That there are factory workers among us who have been thrown out of work by the failures of the global economy is also undeniably important. To show that there is a case for *historical* redress, we would have to show that what was done by the previous managers of our polity has special 'urgency and priority'[21] in relation to other claims. But can any of the arguments that we have considered actually show that? The argument from the intergenerational nature of polities comes close, and in the case of treaties is surely convincing as far as it goes, but otherwise, to the extent that it has to morph into a concern about present injustice, it loses its distinctive appeal and claims. It does not succeed in giving the victims of older injustice any sort of edge over the victims of newer injustice.

So what is the conclusion? It is this: If there is a case for historical redress, it will have to turn on the claim that historical injustice leaves a particular kind of mark that distinguishes it, in some way, from new injustice. The next chapter takes up this thought.

5
BACK TO THE FUTURE

Obviously, we need to take another step, though, before we have a case for historical redress. There are good reasons, the last chapter argued, for thinking that one is complicit in supporting what one's state does, and perhaps this is the best argument going for connecting individual responsibility with collective action. States only work because people support them, and those who support them carry a share in accountability for their acts. Even if you accept all that, however, you only have a reason to think that people are complicit in what their states *do*. It does not immediately make them complicit in what their states once *did*. Sure, there are ideas about the state, in the history of political thought, that represent it as a sort of super-person embracing all generations of its citizens, but I do not believe in them and I would be surprised if many readers of this book gave them much credence either. Complicity has the merit, it was argued above, of being a matter of what people actually do, not of who they are, and for that reason has a better claim to give rise to responsibilities, at least in the context of large and impersonal associations. Lending what is in most cases a very small degree of support to one's state is no doubt a weak example of 'doing', but it is real enough; whereas just being a citizen of a state that performed some vile deed in the seventeenth century is not real enough. All British taxpayers in the early 1980s can be said to have lent some very small degree of support to the Falklands War. But do not try to tell them that they lent any degree of support, even very, very small, to Cromwell's siege of Drogheda in 1649, when thousands of people (soldiers and civilians) in that town in Ireland were slaughtered by his troops, or that they lent support to the brutal suppression of mutiny in British India.

There is a way that we can get to historical redress from political complicity, though, and that is through the idea of *reproduction* – the idea that political systems make decisions about what to pass on to the future. It would be quite an exaggeration to say that the political system that we belong to is responsible for the entire repertoire of social conditions that we live with, a repertoire that is largely inherited, not politically decided (by us, the living); but in making choices about what to do and what not to do – as, of course, it has to, since resources are scarce, and because some options are incompatible – a political system reproduces many of the conditions that it has inherited from the past. In reproducing conditions – as opposed to simply inheriting them – states play an active part, not a passive one. They make decisions. They make decisions about which inherited conditions are acceptable and which are not. And this gives the idea of their citizens' complicity a foothold, if it is true, as argued above, that their citizens can be said to lend support to what states decide to tolerate or else to challenge.

And – another important 'if' – *if* past injustices continue to have an effect in the present. But that leads us straight to the three questions that this chapter will discuss. First, can we clearly show that past injustices *do* continue to have an effect on the present? Second, if we can show that, doesn't that really undermine the whole idea of historical redress – doesn't it show that it is present deprivation, not its historical causes, that should concern us? And third, if we are concerned about present deprivation, can we also show that there is a special obligation to respond to historically caused deprivation, given all the other claims on what states ought to do? (That cannot be the only obligation states have, surely – there are so many other demands on them, some of them quite new.) Let us take these questions in turn.

Inherited wrongs

Do past injustices continue to have an effect in the present? We need to get past something, first of all, that tends to make the claim look

BACK TO THE FUTURE

more implausible than it needs to be. When we think about long-past events (in the seventeenth or eighteenth centuries, say) and things that are going on now, it may at first look as though there is an unbridgeable temporal gap. How, we might ask, can something that is 200 or 300 years old continue to exercise influence in the present? Normally, after all, we want cause and effect to be pretty close in time. If I got bad news this morning (I did not get my pay raise), then it is understandable that I am in a bad mood this afternoon, much less understandable if I got the news in 1960. But the image of a temporal gap is very misleading. A better image would be something like a chain of influences reaching from past to present by way of a series of links eventually reaching the present generation. While the siege of Drogheda is indeed old news (1649 news!), what it expressed – the British government's ruthlessness in regard to the interests of Irish people – continued into the twentieth century, and is hardly improbably remote from the memories of people alive today. Similarly, while slavery was abolished long ago, the end of the US Civil War was by no means the end of the story, and there are African-Americans alive today, for example, who in their youth were violently prevented from exercising their right to vote. (Even more recently, they may have been prevented from voting by more devious means.) That is because, despite the legal abolition of slavery, a set of social and political attitudes has been passed down from generation to generation, in ways that affect both the family memories and the personal experiences of living people.

That does not mean, of course, that we should now set aside the graphic seventeenth- and eighteenth-century episodes of massive violence as being beside the point these days. But it does mean that, instead of being puzzled about how to relate them to the present, or being worried about tenuous long-term causal connections, we should see them as beginnings and emblems of a continuing process. It is surely true that Irish people were more profoundly and generally affected by the potato famine in 1845 than by Cromwell's military campaigns, and perhaps true that the denial of voting rights in the US South after the Civil War is more consequential today than the fact of slavery itself. But it is quite artificial to separate the later parts of the story from the beginning. The beginning is reproduced until it is ended. For the most part, then, we are not really talking about an ancient past, we are talking about a quite recent past with ancient beginnings, and one that it is not mysterious to relate (even in a causal way) to the present. It is better, one commentator has written, to think in terms of 'enduring injustice', as distinct from 'historical injustice', if the second term misleadingly suggests that the injustice lies only in the past.[1] So what, one might ask again, is the reason for looking to the past at all?

The lynching of Louis Sam

The Indian political theorist Rajeev Bhargava has written about the 'cultural injustice' of colonialism, meaning by that the dislocation of people from their traditional frameworks of meaning, as well as their coming to internalize the colonizers' disdain for their way of life. 'Neither economic nor political control could have been sustained without the pervasive belief in the cultural superiority of the colonizers.'[2] The effect, Bhargava claims, can continue through many generations, long after colonization has formally ended in a political sense, and can have a long-term distorting effect on people's perception and behaviour.

Here is a different and particularly graphic example of long-term effect. Only one racial lynching is thought to have taken place in Canada, and it happened in 1884. There was a murder in the village of Nooksack in what is now the State of Washington, just south of the Canadian border. Suspicion fell (wrongly, as it turned out) on Louis Sam, a 14-year-old boy from the aboriginal Sto:lo nation, who had been looking for work in Nooksack on the day in question, but had returned home to his reserve in Canada. On the advice of the local US sheriff, a Canadian magistrate took Sam into custody to await trial; but a gang of armed men from Nooksack crossed the border, seized the boy and hanged him. In 2006, the legislature of the State

BACK TO THE FUTURE 115

of Washington passed a resolution acknowledging the 'unfortunate historical injustice'.

Ten years before that, an article carefully setting out the facts was published by a Canadian historian, Keith Carlson.[3] He had been encouraged to research the incident by elders of the Sto:lo nation

> wishing to put an end to a wave of teenage suicides *by hanging* on Sto:lo reserves, which they linked to the memory of Louis Sam. Clarence Pennier, grand chief of the Sto:lo, made it clear at the ceremony at the Washington State legislature that the Sto:lo have never forgotten Louis Sam's death.[4]

Even if that was, as is believed, the only racial lynching on Canadian soil, it would hardly stand out, among so many and such varied acts of brutality and injustice of the period, if it were not for many other kinds of oppression that the native peoples of the north-west coast and elsewhere endured. Their culture was deliberately undermined, their means of subsistence taken away and their good faith abused. The lynching of Louis Sam would be lost to memory if it were not for all that. After all, English people these days do not in the same way grieve the physical abuse of Captain Jenkins, the cutting off of whose ear even led to a minor war with Spain in 1739. Whatever it was, between England and Spain, that made the loss of his ear a reason (or pretext) for war has now been superseded or (very much more likely) simply forgotten. In contrast, the lynching of Louis Sam is, once again, an emblem of something more systematic and protracted: In this way, it is like the siege of Drogheda, or the particularly horrific way in which Africans were transported in slave ships, or the refusal, in 1939, to land the MS *St Louis*, a ship carrying hundreds of Jewish refugees from Germany, one-third of whom subsequently died in death camps. The particular event gets its meaning from the larger context. But if the Sto:lo elders were right, the particular event continues to exercise a particular kind of effect. Over a century later, it seems, teenage boys of Louis Sam's age continued to internalize not only the violence against him but even its specific and particularly brutal form.[5]

This gives us the best answer to the objection that, if it is present circumstances that worry us, then what is called for is not *historical* redress, but simple justice. The objection has weight if it means that, if it were not for the fact that old injustices had present effects, we would not be concerned about them, or not in a way that demanded redress, at any rate. That is true: Current deprivation is the trigger. But we do need to invoke history, all the same, if we cannot understand current deprivation without it, and if we cannot understand what sort of remedy current deprivation demands without looking into its distant causes. Sure, Louis Sam would just be material for a 'historical' movie if it weren't for teen suicide hangings among his people now; but if we grasp the historical roots of those young people's behaviour, there is no reason not to call the remedy – whatever it is – historical redress. (The remedy is likely to be very complex, and its effects uncertain.) The *liability* for redress arises from what is happening right now – such as a disproportionate suicide rate. The *remedy* is what makes it necessary to look to the past.

Why history matters

So we have two good reasons to take history seriously: one is that a history that began long ago may effectively continue in ways that affect living people's lives, and a second is that the particular character of long-past events may have enduring effects, which we cannot otherwise begin to understand, let alone try to remedy. But that still does not take us quite far enough. True, we may say that in tolerating those effects, political systems reproduce them, in ways that make their members complicit. But political systems reproduce all kinds of things, many of them negative in some way, not just the particular kinds of burden that are carried by the groups that we are concerned with here. Do those burdens stand out in some special way? Or should they just take their place in what, unfortunately, is bound to be a very long queue? And take their chances? Sometimes, it is argued that redressing injuries to historically disadvantaged groups has a certain priority over responding to other inequalities 'because it has the weight of both distributive and corrective justice on its side',[6] that is, it deals with two kinds of injustice at once. But that claim would be more compelling if it were true that other kinds of inequality had their origins exclusively within the lifetimes of those who suffer them, while evidence suggests that they too have a good deal to do with the weight of the past.

Let us say that we favour some moderately progressive social view, according to which over and above some level of well-being that should be guaranteed, improvement of one's circumstances should be within everyone's reach. We are not particularly concerned about equality as such, let us say – that is, we are not objecting to some people ending up better off than others, as long as everyone has a real opportunity to reach the level of fulfilment that they desire. Such a view is quite widely held, in part, it must be admitted, because people can agree to it in principle while disagreeing sharply about where the appropriate level of well-being is. But that does not matter in this context. Let us just say that everyone should have an opportunity to reach . . . (fill in the blank).

Whether or not people do reach the level that we select will depend partly on their circumstances and partly on their choices. This is a distinction that recent political philosophers have made a great deal of.[7] *Circumstances* are things in your situation that would be there because that is the hand that society has dealt you. You make *choices* about how to use the hand that society has dealt you. The importance of the distinction is that while it seems right that people should bear the costs of the choices that they make, it seems completely unfair to make them pay the cost of their unchosen circumstances – that is, the hand that they had to begin with. You shouldn't have to pay for special access to public buildings if you are confined to a wheelchair. You should have to pay for the expensive champagne that you have cultivated a taste for. So we need to distinguish between two streams of advantages and disadvantages in people's lives, in terms of what they are responsible for and what they are not, because the difference is morally important.

Historical redress has generally been seen as a matter of evening up *circumstances*, for obvious enough reasons. History has plainly given some groups a better hand to play with than others have been dealt, and a fair society should recognize this and adopt forms of compensation that level things up, so that groups do not have to go on paying the cost of something that they cannot reasonably be held responsible for having. From this point of view, however, historically deprived groups seem to me to be in exactly the same position as underprivileged individuals, with neither a stronger nor a weaker claim. There is a familiar objection to affirmative action programmes for ethnic groups, programmes that are designed to compensate for past discrimination by requiring preference for their members in hiring decisions, for example, or in admission to professional schools such as law and medicine. The objection, made by or on behalf of less well-off members of the majority community, is that the obstacles faced by them are quite as severe as those faced by minorities; or even – a stronger form of the same objection – that some impoverished members of the majority community are actually *more* disadvantaged than those minority-group individuals who are most likely to benefit from affirmative action policies: for they will be the more advantageously placed members of their group, not the group's worst-off members, for whom the opportunities are too far out of reach to benefit from. I think this objection is right. On the moderately progressive idea of social justice sketched above, disadvantages faced by minority-group members and majority-group members are on exactly the same footing.

So, should we reject affirmative action policies? No, because (perhaps surprisingly) the case for them may make more headway if we turn from *circumstances* to the question of *choice*. In a society that values equal opportunity rather than absolute equality, much of

BACK TO THE FUTURE

anyone's fate is going to depend on their ability to participate in those processes through which valuable things get to be distributed – social, economic and political processes. People differ greatly in terms of their ability to participate in those processes – in terms of their assertiveness, for example, their horizons of possibility, the demandingness of their expectations for themselves, their background knowledge of how institutions work. The deepest effects of historical injustice are those that influence such things: negative effects on self-image that damage the idea that one can hope to participate with success. Sociologists speak of 'the sense of efficacy', and that captures exactly the value that historical injustice can undermine. If teenage boys in reservations on Canada's Pacific coast see themselves, at some deep level, as victims of lynching, their life choices may shrink to the point that they become death choices.

The example, I hope, helps to make the point that talk about 'choice' does not imply – as it often does – endorsement of a consumer culture in which choice among (largely similar) goods becomes a value. Valuing choice does not carry with it any judgement about what is chosen, still less any idea that more choice is better. If members of oppressed minorities want to assimilate to and enjoy the opportunities of the majority society, all well and good. Certainly, we need to distinguish between groups of people whose members typically want to join majority society, and groups whose members typically want to preserve their identity from its influences. But protecting choice also means removing the stigma from any choice that is made, including a decision to reject the values of consumer culture and to assert a traditional identity. If what is important is that people should feel that they are 'self-originating sources of valid claims' (to quote a famous liberal political philosopher[8]), that must mean that they have a sense of *self* that is not weakened by the status of the group that they identify with; that who they are does not somehow invalidate who they want to be. The overriding idea is that people should be capable of framing the course of their lives, not in a way that owes nothing to history, but in a way that is undistorted by the persistent effects of oppression.

But don't we now face exactly the same objection as the 'even up circumstances' proposal? That it is not only minority-group members whose sense of efficacy may be impaired, that within majority society, social class can have pretty well identical effects? A fine work of sociology, *The Hidden Injuries of Class*, makes precisely that point, tracing the ways in which blue-collar workers in the United States come to accept limited horizons of ambition entirely different from those of their more highly educated middle-class fellow citizens.[9] And surely this is true. But it is here that the element of reproduction comes to be especially significant. There are compelling reasons to think that historically caused damage to minorities, while no worse than the injuries of class – and how could we really measure that? – is much more likely to be reproduced unless special measures are taken.

While societies such as ours are very far from achieving equality of any kind, even the modest equality-of-opportunity version, they are permeated by the language of equality. While privilege certainly exists on an enormous scale, the language of privilege does not, and no proposal, no programme, no candidate for political office, would survive for a moment by adopting it. Built into the way we do things, and justify them publicly, there is a powerful egalitarian trend – differently understood, to be sure, as noted above – that works against class-differentiated opportunities. No doubt it works more slowly than many readers of this book would like, but it is there, presenting class-based inequalities with a standing principled obstacle.

Historical injustice, however, is something that we cannot identify by means of any sort of abstract principle. We have to know what actually happened. History did not have to happen the way that it did, and if what happened came to be lost, we could not somehow reconstruct it from first principles, like the propositions of geometry, which we could if necessary recover if somehow all the textbooks came to be burned by an anti-Euclidian government: unlike the properties of triangles, 'Everything that actually happened in the realm of human affairs could just as well have been otherwise.'[10] Unless brute fact – the siege of Drogheda, the lynching of Louis Sam, the turning away of the *St Louis* – is remembered, it will vanish, and whatever it is that descends from those facts will become inexplicable and so uncompensable, and its effects unrecognizable. Here, I think, we have at last arrived at an argument for the unique importance of historical redress. It would be unsupportable, and even insulting to some, to claim that the historic suffering of minorities is somehow worse than the disadvantages experienced by all those who are on the losing end of current economic arrangements. But there is still a case for saying that the brute facts of history, and their current effects on minorities' participation in society, will be lost to sight unless they are deliberately and publicly recalled. So recalling them, in whatever is the most appropriate and effective way, should be the aim of redress.

There is another important distinction to be made, too. If we think of social class in terms of a systematically unequal distribution of benefits and opportunities, the point, from a position that values equality, is, obviously, to get rid of it. It is simply not a good thing that societies should be divided in that way. It makes a mockery of equal opportunity; for even if individual members of underprivileged classes can escape from them, they cannot all do so, unless classes cease to exist. Some people are content with a weak idea of equal opportunity that requires only the chance of mobility from one class to another, but in presupposing the existence of classes that weak idea obviously denies opportunities to more people than it grants them to.[11] (It is a bit like saying that we all have an equal opportunity to win the lottery if we buy a ticket – true, but the pay-out necessarily presupposes many more losing than winning tickets.) So a stronger idea of equal opportunity calls for the elimination of class. But it does not in the same way call for the elimination of ethnic groups that have suffered injustice in the past; it certainly calls for removing whatever handicaps can be traced to that injustice, but the point, far from being the destruction of the group itself, is to allow its members to assert their identity, if they wish, with more confidence and freedom. Doing that has a value that is distinct from finding a remedy for social and economic inequality in general. And doing that requires history.

Ants and grasshoppers

Even if you accept the argument above, however, there is still a further question lurking in the background. Suppose we all agree that historical injustices continue to exercise profound effects, and that while there is no basic reason to give them more of our concern than other injustices should get, there is much more of a chance that they will be reproduced, given that their origins – in contingent facts – will be lost unless publicly and emphatically remembered: suppose we accept all that, why is it so important that injustice should not be reproduced? Injustice is bad, we can all agree, but is there some sort of special badness in reproducing it?

There is, and to see why we need to go back to the topic discussed in Chapter 1 – the topic of rights. We looked at the question of whether non-existent people could be said to have rights, and we noted the objection that deceased people cannot have rights because they cannot benefit from them. Future people, although currently non-existent, can have rights on this argument, however, because at some point in the future, if and when they come to be, they will be capable of benefiting from them and experiencing the benefits. Now it may seem odd to go back to that topic when we are trying to see if there is a case for historical redress; but it becomes relevant now that we are focusing on the reproduction of historical injustice, as something that present generations can be held responsible for. For the conditions that present generations reproduce will obviously affect the rights of future generations, if indeed future generations do have rights.

The last thing that we need to work out, then, is how the reproduction of historical injustice damages some right that future people may have. The right that is damaged is one that we could call *the right to clarity*, and it is one that has a special importance in the context of the idea of justice that we are relying on here.

In an equal opportunity society, as we have seen, what happens in people's lives is determined in part by their own choices, or by the

BACK TO THE FUTURE

use that they make of the resources at their disposal. The outcome of those choices can be said to be just, but only on one condition: that the resources at their disposal in the first place are justly held. If you and I each begin with a fair share of resources, and you invest yours prudently (high-return ethical investments) while I spend mine building a pointless gilded replica of the Eiffel Tower, our very different circumstances 10 years later can be justified in terms of our personal responsibility for our choices. In terms of Aesop's famous fable, you were the Ant, I was the Grasshopper, and so it is quite all right that you should be comfortably off while I am not. (If you prefer an alternative fable, you were the Little Red Hen who planted the wheat and baked the bread, I was her free-loader friend, the Dog or the Pig, who expected to eat the bread without contributing to it.[12]) We have to know, though, before accepting this justification, that there was nothing wrong with the holdings that we started with. We rely almost entirely on social and legal institutions to confirm this for us, for otherwise the task of investigating where things come from would be all consuming. But we also want to feel pretty sure that the social and legal institutions that assign ownership of things are not purely arbitrary in their results, that some principle of fairness underlies them. I can feel justified in building my gilded Eiffel Tower replica only if I am confident that the resources I am using should not really be in the hands of someone else; likewise, you can claim credit for the more prudent use of your holdings only if you can show that you began with your fair share of resources. It is this that I am calling a 'right to clarity'. And there are at least three ways in which this right may involve historical redress.

First, and most obviously, people may have holdings – of land, or capital – that were unjustly seized. Although this is the most obvious way in which the question of redress arises, it is not, in many cases, a very conclusive one, for all the reasons that we discussed in earlier chapters. While the injustice should certainly be remembered in whatever is the most fitting way, it is not always clear that the right thing to do is simply to give back what was taken, given all that has happened between then and now, and the new expectations that possession has created. I do think it needs to be said, though, that we have to be satisfied that the reasons for rejecting the return of what was seized really are good reasons, not just conveniently self-serving ones. So even if return is not the right thing to do, historical injustice continues to pose a moral problem that should oblige us to think about the right thing to do and critically weigh the arguments for retaining what was seized. For the considerations may sometimes change. The discovery of a burial place, for example, may show that a piece of land was not just an economic resource for native people but a place of irreplaceable spiritual importance, so that the claim for return is that much more compelling. Or, if a piece of land was expropriated from a native band for military purposes during the Second World War, the justification becomes empty 65 years after the war has ended. There is a permanent challenge based on dispossession, even though the challenge may often be defeated, for the time being at least, by good reasons.

Second, a less obvious consideration, but one that may be more generally promising: Things that inhibit participation by minorities confer an unearned advantage on majorities. We don't need to make a fetish of competition, as free-market advocates sometimes do, to recognize that as a matter of course there is competition for valued things: lucrative and prestigious employment, for example, or necessarily scarce places in professional schools, or scholarships. If there are factors, grounded in history, that discourage minorities from aspiring for such things, or from competing effectively for them, that gives a sort of additional resource to members of the majority. It is a bit like getting hold of a monopoly in trade – you get to have an advantage that tops up whatever merit you may have. This argument is also very much like an argument developed powerfully by John Stuart Mill, the nineteenth-century liberal philosopher, in his book *The Subjection of Women*. At present, he says, men compete with each other in a pool of competitors that is almost exactly half as big as it would be if women were socially and legally authorized to enter it, and if they had the educational opportunities that equipped them to do so. So each man has on average about twice the competitive power that can be attributed to whatever can be called his merit. The case of minorities whose historical experience impedes participation is exactly parallel. So if members of the majority society are to be and to feel justified in possessing the resources that they have, they should accept policies that help to restore the competitive position of minorities. If these are affirmative action policies – policies giving minorities an edge in competition for scarce and valued things – they would be justified as our best (and necessarily approximate) guess as to where minority candidates would be ranked if the history of their group could somehow be discounted.[13] There are several other justifications for affirmative action policies, but they are much more open to objection.

Third, there is a consideration that may be the most important of all, though what it calls for in practice may seem unsettled. If we are to be able to assess the justice of the way things are, we need to have an undistorted understanding of how societies work and change. If we believe that merit is rewarded and that failure results from the lack of merit; that some groups lack merit because of their endowment, cultural or genetic, or, alternatively, that anyone can succeed if they only try; that history is a simple line of progress in which there are pure gains, no real losses; that history's losers deserved to lose; that criticism of the way things are expresses nothing but resentment at not being a winner – if we believe all this, or any of it, then we are in no position to make realistic judgements about the fairness of the starting-points that people have in societies like ours. If we believe all this, or any of it, it means that we are blind to the operation of power in the way that historical change occurs. If historical redress in some form – most likely in effectively symbolic form – is the way to bring home to us the fact of power, and its consequences, then it is nothing less than essential to the way in which societies such as ours are justified. We need to know how we came to have what we have, and we need to know how society works if we are to make fair judgements about the future. If we sweep historical injustices aside, our chances of reaching any sort of clear understanding of how societies work are close to zero.

On clarity

In saying that there is a *right* to clarity – about how people came to occupy the positions that they do occupy, and about the nature of historical and social processes in general – the point is of course to try to bring into the argument the power of the idea of 'a right' that was outlined earlier in Chapter 1. Rights – if they can be successfully argued for – are, as we saw, enormously powerful things, outweighing other things that are simply 'interests' of a personal kind or else projects that would be convenient in terms of public policy. If I have a property right in my back garden, that means that you cannot enter it even if you are deeply interested in observing the unusual beetle that lives there (unless I allow you to), and if I have a right to a fair trial that means that the sheriff has to give me one, even if it would be very much simpler (and cheaper) to give in to the armed and angry lynch mob waiting outside the jail. As these examples suggest, we tend to think of rights in terms of tangible or measurable things such as property and security. That is certainly where the idea of rights emerged, as a way of resisting oppressive monarchical power with designs on the freedoms and the belongings of subjects. So isn't a right to *clarity* a bit mysterious? How can we count something intangible among those basic interests, like personal security, that normally form the basis of rights? Doing so seems doubly questionable, moreover, if in the name of a supposed right to clarity we adopt measures of redress that may sometimes diminish the tangible resources that the majority enjoys, by, for example, making compensatory payments, or extending to minorities opportunities that majorities do not enjoy.

All the same, there is a case for believing that such a right is enormously important, and that if it is not often invoked, it is because it operates at a level that is often below that of consciousness.

BACK TO THE FUTURE 127

Imaginative philosophical or artistic efforts are sometimes needed to bring it to light. The (particularly imaginative) philosopher Robert Nozick came up with a famous example, that of 'the experience machine'.[14] Suppose there was a machine, he says, that we could hook ourselves up to, and which would then give us the experience of doing something wonderfully pleasurable even though we were not really doing it – we could have the experience of being an Alpine ski champion, for example, or a supreme creative artist like Cervantes or Rembrandt – all without putting on skis or writing *Don Quixote* or painting 'The Night Watch', or having the skills you need to do any of those things. Would it matter that we were living an illusion? Another example, from film: In the movie *The Truman Show*, the title character discovers that his placidly contented life is in fact part of a highly scripted soap opera, that family, friends and neighbours are skilled actors, and that his idyllic little town is actually a movie set encased in an impermeable bubble. No one who sees that movie, as far as I know, regrets Truman's eventual discovery of the reality, even though it causes him a good deal of grief. If that would be your response too, and if you are also repelled by the idea of life in an experience machine, then you may see the point and the value of having clarity about one's situation. We just want to know. Moreover, what we do not know about ourselves limits our capacity to act – this is the bedrock truth of psychoanalysis – and can also corrupt our connections with others. To quote Bernhard Schlink again, 'If something is wrong with one's biography, then one's sense of self and also one's relationships with others will suffer.'[15]

Clarity may not always be a priority, or perhaps even desirable. An ingenious counter-example: suppose Mrs Smith gives birth in a hospital, and due to some careless mix-up by the nursing staff, she and Mr Smith go home with someone else's baby, believing it to be their own.[16] The Smiths are model parents, bringing up 'their' child with care and affection, all the while believing her or him to be biologically related to them, a belief that the child eventually comes to share. All is well with the Smiths. But then the truth comes to light – perhaps an officious hospital administrator comes across a discrepancy in the records. Should she phone the Smiths with the news? Let us set aside cases in which some hereditary physical condition is involved that would make it medically necessary to tell the truth, cases that, while important, distract us from the point here. Would not most people think it unnecessary, or even perhaps wrong, to dispel the Smiths' illusion? Now David Miller, the inventor of this parable, points out that the Smiths' belief in their biological connection with their child is only a 'background' belief (i.e. one that supports their practices, but one that could be replaced, indifferently, by others) as opposed to a 'constitutive' belief (i.e. one that is indispensable to their practices); for example, the belief that someone likes you is constitutive of your friendship with him or her, and evidence that he or she does not destroys the relationship. In the case of 'constitutive' beliefs, truth is obviously important, and falsehood should be brought to light, as may not be the case with background beliefs. The beliefs that we are concerned with are clearly of the second kind. If people believe, for example, that social and economic standing owe nothing to past injustice but simply reflect personal merit, that belief will enter, in a constitutive way, into their relations with others and into policies to which they give political support. So will their belief that the circumstances of others are natural rather than historical in origin.

But is our interest in clarity so important that we can be said to have a right to it? There are three standard tests for rights. First, are the interests that they protect important ones? Second, is it feasible to protect them? Third, are the potential rights 'generalizable', to use the term that philosophers have invented – that is to say, is it possible that the right could be exercised by everyone (not just by me at your expense, or by you at my expense)? If you accept that there is an important interest in clarity, as the previous paragraphs tried to show, then the 'right to clarity' passes the other two tests with flying colours. It can hardly be unfeasible to provide people with clarity about their circumstances – it is not like promising everyone a holiday home in the Adriatic, a promise that would quickly run up against physical

BACK TO THE FUTURE

constraints: There is enough clarity to go round, unlike pieces of the Adriatic coast. Likewise, it is hard to see how my possession of clarity would diminish yours, or yours mine. In fact, it is a particularly good example of something that people could enjoy without diminishing others' supply of it. So I do not see that anything stands in the way of talking about a right to clarity.

Outside the minds of philosophers (and movie scriptwriters), however, does this supposed right have a place? There are some real-world examples, varied in their usefulness here. There are examples of cases where people's interests are damaged because they are misinformed – voters induced by propaganda to support policies that are actually very bad for them – but those would not really do for the present purpose, because we need cases in which clarity is important for its own sake, not for the sake of something else, such as coming to see what one's own real interests are. We come very close in the case of governments justifying foreign policies or wars on the basis of disinformation, something that electorates deeply resent when truth comes to light, even though the damage has mainly been inflicted on people in other countries – they do not like being 'had'. We come closer still if we consider the general distaste for lying in public life; the penalties exacted for lying, which are often worse than the penalties for whatever it was that was lied about; the value here is one that is attached to audits, to the disclosure of information and to mechanisms that make disclosure likely, such as media that are not politically controlled. None of this would make sense unless we thought it important to be undeceived about what is going on around us; perhaps, again, because it is important for reasons to do with protecting our interests, but more likely – if we consider the moral revulsion that deception provokes – because we are insulted and demeaned when the truth is hidden from us: and saying that we have a right to clarity is one way to express this.

It is unusual, no doubt, to put historical redress into this category of things, along with public audits, freedom of information and a politically independent press. It is more usual to think of it in terms of restorative justice, along with apology and reconciliation, or else distributive justice, as a righting of distributive wrongs such as unjustified inequalities; or even retributive justice, as a matter of attaching blame to someone for some wrongful act. We have discussed such views in this book, and I hope to have made a case that if we want a distinctive argument for historical redress, one that attaches a special kind of importance to it, we should value it, rather, as one of the things that contributes to social clarity, and hence as something that we owe to future generations. It is a sort of historical audit. We become responsible for myths and deceptions about the past – even though we did not create them – by reproducing them, and we carry out our responsibility for past injustice by acknowledging it adequately and explaining it in ways that allow future generations to understand how things came to be, and how they came to live the lives that they have inherited.

CONCLUSION

In this short book, I have argued that while the case for historical redress is compelling in many ways, it confronts one problem above all – a problem of responsibility. No doubt it would be good if past evils and evils inherited from the past, and indeed new evils too, could be responded to, in any way that seems possible and right. But there are many things that it would be good to do, without anyone's having the responsibility to do them. Why are we – English people born long after the Irish potato famine, German people born after the end of Naziism, American people who never enslaved anyone, Japanese people who never treated prisoners cruelly – responsible for making up for what our ancestors did? Or, more exactly, for what some of our co-citizens' ancestors did, if we or our families immigrated after the events in question occurred?

We looked at some proposed answers to this question: the idea that the rights of those who suffered continue in force after their death; the idea that being in possession of benefits make us liable for how the benefits were acquired; the idea that there is a duty of memory; the idea that a duty of redress is somehow implicit in who we (collectively) are. All of these ideas, while not without attractions, were questioned, although the last one, in one of its versions, pointed towards the answer that was eventually defended in Chapter 5. As citizens, it was argued, we are complicit in what is done by the political systems that we support; while that still does not make us complicit in what *was* done by those systems in the past, it does make us complicit in the reproduction of the effects of past evils. Our responsibility, then, lies in not reproducing those effects; and it arises from a right enjoyed by future generations, that is, a right to live lives untainted by avoidable injustice and unmystified by false accounts of how things came to be. That is the paradox mentioned in the Introduction – that historical redress is best justified by future people's rights. But I think it is only an apparent paradox. The present generation, after all, as the moment between past and future generations, is the medium by which the past is selectively transmitted to the future, and has responsibilities that arise from that very basic fact. How could it not be so?

In the course of this book, we have looked at theories of redress in the light of various examples. But to round off the discussion, I would like to return to the list of examples that was used to get it launched in the Introduction. What, after the thoughts offered in this book, can we make of them?

1. We began with the case of the Elgin (Parthenon) Marbles, such a famous case that it has given rise to the word 'Elginism', meaning the construction of arguments for retaining something that was wrongly or dubiously or contentiously acquired. (Pick your own adverb.) A full discussion of the pros and cons of that particular long-standing and much-debated case would take far more space than is available here. But considering the case just as an example, it has to be said that, on the basis of the arguments developed in this book, it falls somewhat short, despite its fame, of the clearest case for return. Returning a prized object can be part of a process of acknowledging and publicly clarifying the past, in a way that changes (for the better!) the relationship between two parties. Beyond the intrinsic value of the object itself to its original possessor, the act of returning it expresses the end of a relationship of domination of one party over the other. The clearest case is that of the return of sacred objects and human remains to aboriginal societies. The point at issue here – a point about equality – was graphically made by the writer Tony Hillerman, in whose novel *Talking God* a (white) lawyer, representing a museum holding native remains, arrives at work to find her own grandparents' skeletons dumped on her desk.

But there has not been a history of domination between Britain and Greece. Twice, in fact, Britain has acted to protect Greece from domination, the first occasion (in the 1820s) being among the earliest instances of what came to be called 'humanitarian intervention', when public opinion in Britain impelled the government to give Greece military aid against the Ottoman Empire,[1] the second occasion being the attempt to defend Crete, and to aid Greek partisans, in the Second World War. Ironically, the first occasion was inspired by exactly the 'philhellenism' that had led Lord Elgin to 'rescue' the Marbles just a few years before – the British loved Greece too much. It is true that he removed them (or so he claimed) with the permission of the Ottoman Sultan (of whose empire Greece was then part), so that although their removal was not an act of British imperialism, it could still be seen as one of Ottoman imperialism, thus expressing Greece's history of imperial subjection all the same. But that makes the injustice of the British Museum's possession of them quite a bit more indirect, and, being really strict and legalistic about the matter, no former empire seems to have any sort of duty to make redress for the misdeeds of other former empires. When the British ransacked the museum collections of the former Ashanti Empire in what is now Ghana, should they have returned the items to the subject peoples from whom they had been taken?[2]

But is it really redress that is the issue? Is it the wrongness of the transfer that is at issue, or, rather, some principle that cultural objects have a sort of natural home in their place of origin? Would the case for return weaken if the Marbles had been purchased in a consensual market transaction, or given away by a weak Greek regime? If so, then the argument for return implies nothing less than the nationalization of art works. It would imply that the sale of art to foreigners was wrong, and perhaps that art should not even be privately owned, if that would restrict all co-nationals' access to it as a national possession. Not only is that a more stringent view than many would endorse, it does not even seem to lead to desirable results. As Anthony Appiah has argued, what is often called the universal value of art does not speak in favour of confining it to its birthplace.[3] Perhaps, then, it is the one-way direction of appropriation that is objectionable, rather than, simply, the relocation of objects from one place to another? But again, that sort of objectionableness would more clearly arise in the case of colonizer/colony relations or the like, rather than in the case of Britain and Greece.

After all that, I would argue for the Marbles' return, all the same, but on the basis of one of the more subsidiary arguments in this book. There is no case in terms of restoring relations between Britain and Greece. There is no real case for the necessary connection between art objects and the national soil on which they were produced. Surely the best case for return depends on neither of those, but on the Marbles' connection with the most iconic representation of Greek identity and of Greece's contribution to the civilization of Europe, the Parthenon. That uniquely important connection means that we have to take account of the issue of respective stakes, or measures of significance. We sometimes allow that issue to weigh, for example, against aboriginal land claims: Whatever the treaty said, the thousands of people who have built their lives around their possession of formerly aboriginal land have a stake in retaining it that cannot be swept aside. By parity of reasoning, surely we have to weigh what Greece would gain, and what the British Museum would lose, by the Marbles' return. Of course, this has to be an on-balance kind of argument. But there seems to be no alternative to that kind of argument when no all-or-nothing principles are available.

On two counts, however, the argument above would seem to demand the return of artefacts from museums to aboriginal people. Not only is it clearly the case that their retention does express a relationship of domination, but also the 'stakes' consideration applies too, and very powerfully. There is no comparison between their meaning for people viewing them in museums and their meaning for their original possessors, especially when the objects embody important cultural or religious references. All the stronger, of course, for both reasons, is the case for returning aboriginal remains, as various museums around the world have done in the past few years, including, for example, the Natural History Museum in London which, in 2011, returned 138 sets of skeletal remains to the Torres Strait Islands (Australia), responding to the Islanders' long campaign for their recovery.

2. The second item on our initial list was the return of land to those who were dispossessed of it. When we consider the current circumstances of those who were dispossessed, two centuries or so ago, it simply cannot be legitimate, surely, to turn a blind eye to their claims. The question, of course, is what they now have a claim *to*. Here the various arguments considered in this book lead to varied results. The main conclusion of Chapter 1 was that it makes sense to speak of violations of 'rights' surviving in cases in which the rights that were violated remain current. We no longer care about violations of rights that we no longer think have a good basis (such as the 'violation' of slave owners' rights when slaves were freed). So whether or not the violation of aboriginal peoples' rights survives depends very much on our thoughts about what their rights were, and are.

Aboriginal people were subjected to physical violence and deception that violated their most basic security rights. If a time-travelling criminal court could visit the eighteenth century and prosecute the government officials, military officers and out-of-control settlers who were responsible, justice could be done. Even at the time in question, decent people had the same standards of justice as us: perhaps the most famous major act of dispossession, of the Cherokee people in 'The Trail of Tears' of 1830, was approved in the US Senate by only one vote, after discussion in the course of which some of the most famous figures in the politics of the time expressed opposition. Since we have no court on the time-travelling circuit, however, we have to consider alternatives. Some alternatives to retribution were discussed above, and we will return to them for some final remarks in commenting on other examples below.

But aboriginal grievances go beyond the acts of violence and deception that led to their dispossession, acts that are rightly to be condemned by whatever appropriate means are available. For often, it is the bare fact (rather than only the means) of dispossession that is grieved, and the grievance is cast in terms of aboriginal peoples' cultural relation to the land that they lost, and the connection of their identity to it. Within that frame of thinking, land is not just an economic resource that owners can buy and sell, but the common resource, invested with cultural and spiritual meaning, of a people. But what should we make of this, in light of the argument that was put forward in Chapter 1?

Violations survive, it was argued there, because ideas of rights do. The majority society has no reason, on that argument, to give weight to violations of those rights that do not accord with their general idea of justice. Now ideas about the just tenure of land change radically from time to time.[4] European societies themselves underwent a radical shift from feudal ideas of land tenure to capitalist ones. Whether or not and to what extent that was a good thing can certainly be discussed. But those who would benefit from a return to feudal systems of land tenure do not have a claim based simply on the fact of their loss. By analogy, then, we can appreciate what aboriginal views mean to those who hold them, without however accepting that they must lead to a case for return. When it comes to a matter of recognizing rights, societies have to act on their own conceptions of the just ownership of things. The idea of rights gets its force from the need to protect people from acts of injustice: and while the violence of dispossession remains plainly unjust, the bare fact of dispossession does not, given that ideas of just possession are not unchangeable. And if it did remain unjust, correcting it (fully) would of course call for a reverse act of unjust dispossession.

That view has been advanced in a frank and forceful way by the political philosopher Jeremy Waldron.[5] It has met with at least two strong criticisms. The first is that, given what is at stake, it is morally and politically dubious to criticize, on philosophical grounds, the few resources that aboriginal people can use to wrest some benefits for themselves from the majority society. Their circumstances, in the settler societies of North America and Australasia, are generally wretched, their lives worse (on average) than the majority's on every index of health, well-being, education and amenities. They are a permanent political minority that will never wield power, and have no natural coalition partners. All they have at their disposal are the legal

CONCLUSION

and rhetorical weapons arising from their historical dispossession, and to criticize these is to obstruct their struggle for justice without offering them any alternative means.[6] The issue here is somewhat parallel to the one discussed in Chapter 2, where we noted opposition to the use of lawsuits that had some practical use even though from a philosophical point of view they might seem to miss the point: Should political philosophers be political first and philosophers after, or the other way around? That issue goes far beyond the scope of this book, and I offer no comment. But we should note that even the critical view depends fundamentally on accepting current measures of injustice, in order to make its case for tolerating imperfect remedies for it. Aboriginal people suffer deprivation according to standards widely adopted in majority society itself: that is why (it is claimed) we should be reluctant to unpick their case. It is, then, ultimately a present-deprivation view of the sort described in Chapter 5, even though it accepts claims based on historical entitlements as important political ways of seeking a solution.

The second criticism is different in that it simply challenges the view that a single conception of justice applies to both the majority society and aboriginal minorities, on the grounds that aboriginal groups see themselves, and should be seen as, independent societies. So the fact that ideas of property current within majority society itself do not give weight to historical entitlement is beside the point: *their* ideas of property do, and *their* ideas include a notion of a collective and cultural tie to land. So it is not just a matter of trying to deal with what everyone knows is wrong on any measure – with some allowance for history-based appeals to be thrown in, out of political fairness – but a matter of basic disagreement about criteria of ownership, and of the relation between a society and the land that it occupies.

Since this disagreement concerns, in part, the same pieces of land, and since (on this line of thinking) there is no common principle to settle the matter, the solution will presumably have to be a negotiated one, in which those whose interests are at stake express their different views and hope to arrive at a resolution that they can all live with. One commentator gives graphic expression to this idea by referring to a wonderful piece of sculpture by a Canadian aboriginal artist, Bill Reid, which depicts a canoe occupied by different creatures (bears, a beaver, an eagle, a frog . . .) who must find some way of cohabiting despite their varied ways of being.[7] This is an appealing image, one that captures the depth of difference, although perhaps one may wonder how far the discussion will get without ground rules of any kind. And establishing the ground rules may require the various parties to stand back from their given identities and think about what is fair. They will need to know, for example, who gets to be at the table: Among the aboriginal communities, do women and young people, urban and reserve inhabitants, get representation that cuts across the divisions between peoples and bands? Within the majority society, do recent immigrants and people of minority religions get representation that introduces their distinctive perspectives? What is a fair decision-rule for arriving at conclusions? Is size of population reflected in voting weight? What is the default position if no conclusion is reached? I do not know how to resolve these issues, but the point is that one can question whether the parties can arrive at answers to them without searching for some principled view that, they believe, other parties should accept.[8]

Whichever of these two views is taken, it seems inescapable, on the rights-based argument, that current ideas of justice will play a crucial role. It is quite true, of course, that we need to keep separate the claims arising from the injustice of dispossession – claims about what people lost – from the claims arising from the injustice of oppression – claims about what people suffered. They amount to distinct grounds. As one writer, discussing a different case, has put it,

> Early Zionist territorial demands concerned the claim for reinstating a state of affairs in which Jews were in control of the land of Israel. They were not seeking compensation for Jewish losses throughout two thousand years of exile from that land.[9]

CONCLUSION

The writer goes on to say that those losses, culminating in the Holocaust, 'hastened the formation of the state of Israel' but did not form 'the moral basis for Zionist territorial aspirations'. Now one might think that those losses did play something of a role in the moral thinking of at least some Zionists; but what is more to the point, it is inconceivable that, without them, the formation and survival of Israel could have won the degree of outside support or even forbearance that it did. Likewise, the moral weight of aboriginal claims today would be very much weaker if all aboriginal people had drinkable water, decent housing and health care, education of a sort that matched their aspirations and a life expectancy similar to that of the larger society. That is not to say that their condition is wrong for material reasons only, but it is to say that it is the injustice of their material circumstances that rightly forces their claims into the public arena.

On balance, then, I think the rights-based view will tend towards a conclusion that is sceptical about demands based on history and ideas of identity bound up with it, and that will tend strongly in favour of responding to present injustice, as the majority society views it. But of course, the rights-based view is only one of several that we need to take into account.

3. Our third case again involved aboriginal peoples – the residential school issue – but also victims of wartime atrocity, of apartheid, and of heavy-handed internment practices. The list could have been made very much longer, for literally hundreds of state actions and policies have given rise to demands for redress of various kinds. Let us stay with the aboriginal case for a moment, though, in order to make the first point that needs to be made.

The residential school episode in North America and Australasia involved many criminal acts, and many acts that would have counted as crimes if not carried out by states – they would be called kidnapping, fraudulent deception and forcible confinement.[10] But it was unlike an ordinary crime, not only in its scale – some 150,000 children passed through residential schools in Canada alone – but also in that it expressed and carried forward a sustained policy of oppression.

Whereas a crime is an exceptional event, a disruption of order, the residential schools formed a *normal* part of a prolonged process in which the interests of aboriginal people were systematically damaged. In that sense, it was all of a piece with their original dispossession, with the disrespect of many of the treaties that were signed with them, and with the current neglect of basic amenities on the much-diminished lands remaining to them. More than that, as a deliberate and explicit attempt to eliminate aboriginal societies by assimilating their children, it was the clearest possible expression (short of physical elimination) of the view that they had no place in the continents controlled by settlers. To understand the episode, then, we have to know not only what happened but what it *meant*.

Something similar needs to be said about the other cases in the list here. To Southeast Asian peoples, their treatment by their Japanese conquerors was an example of the chronic contempt with which they were regarded. The apartheid regime was only one relatively brief phase in the relations between the races in South Africa. The internment of people of Japanese descent in the Second World War reflected pervasive racism in the societies into which they had immigrated. So what is of overriding importance in responding, after the fact, to these events, is that the means adopted should bring out to the fullest possible extent their meaning within the histories that they form part of. Here truth commissions would seem to have an unrivalled value as a way of bringing out the story that needs to be told. They are not in this respect inferior, a second-best, to criminal trials, for their storytelling power is much greater. We need to acknowledge that they have truth-telling power in only a limited sense, as noted in Chapter 3, in that (to be honest) we know in advance – as good historians should not already know – which parts of the truth are to be foregrounded in the completed record. But from the point of view defended in Chapter 5, the truth commission could not be more appropriate: If what we want to avoid, above all, is the reproduction of injustice, then we need to create as compelling an account of it as we can and to place it immovably on the public record. The truth commission and

CONCLUSION

the international criminal tribunal are the twentieth century's main contributions to historical redress. Despite differences, they are similar in their ambition to elevate the victim's status in the name of restoring a conception of equality.

Compensation, the other resource discussed at this point in our initial list, is another story. Here I set aside the question of compensation to living survivors, which surely falls into its own category. The living survivors of residential schools, victims of the brutality of the apartheid regime, the remaining 'comfort women', and those who suffered at British hands in the Kenya 'emergency', deserve compensation not as a way of wiping away what they were subjected to but as a way, simply, of remedying the harm done. If what they went through had been suffered at the hands of private individuals, they would, unquestionably, have had legal recourse against those who inflicted the wrongs. That it was, in their case, a state that inflicted the wrongs, cannot make a moral difference, and the state's liability to compensate is no more mysterious than my duty to compensate the person whose car I back into in the supermarket parking lot (especially if I backed into it deliberately). Money is, obviously, less perfect a remedy than in the case of property damage, but it is (sometimes) the only material remedy available. Compensation to the deceased (or their later descendants), however, is not so obviously right, as we have seen. For some conclusions about this, let us turn to the next item in the list.

4. Holocaust reparations are sometimes seen as the paradigm case of compensation – one that has certainly inspired successor cases – but they can be seen in several ways. Some survivors still lived, and millions had suffered the death of close relatives, so the redress was not quite 'historical' if that is taken to mean that the losses were suffered by past generations. (Perhaps we could take it to be historical in the somewhat weaker sense, though, that the events in question definitively ended with the total defeat of the Nazi regime.) If we think of them as compensation to living people or immediate relatives, then (as suggested just above) they resemble the damages awarded by courts in civil cases, and to that extent are uncontentious.

Second, the German payments to Israel were officially described as payments for the cost of resettling millions of refugees from Europe: so they could be seen as the equivalent of the much older category of 'war debts', such as those imposed on Germany at Versailles in 1919, debts measured by the cost to the victims of aggression. In that light, they look like a late example of something very old rather than the precursor of a new moral regime. Third, the payments, whatever they meant to those who received them, amounted to a substantial burden to the post-war (West) German state, and so could be seen as a sort of self-imposed fine, important primarily as an acknowledgement of guilt. That is clearly implied in the view that the lesson of reparations was that 'crimes of genocide cannot go unpunished and the moral debt arising must be paid'.[11] The payment is a sort of punishment to the payer.

As it happens, the payments (made in hard currency), as well as representing a loss to Germany, were also of great value to the emerging and cash-strapped Israeli state. Despite that, as noted in the Introduction, many Israelis vehemently opposed accepting them, fearing that they represented an attempt to 'whitewash' the past by a display of generosity, or by buying off the victims. That would have been a reasonable suspicion, given that there was something disturbing in the very idea that any amount of money could be seen as making good the suffering that the Nazi regime caused. But if anything gives the payments moral validity it is that they were followed by, and possibly helped to bring about, a process of national soul-searching in Germany that was unprecedented in European history.[12] No other society has made such efforts to face up to the past and to try to ensure that the lessons would not be forgotten by the young and by later generations. Seen in that light – but perhaps only when seen in that light – the compensation payments show up well. That may suggest that the 'self-imposed fine' interpretation is preferable to the 'war debt' interpretation.

So compensation fits well into the general argument of this book, if seen in a forward-looking way. It is one way of making and declaring a break with past actions, a step beyond making a purely verbal promise. But I am not sure that that view of it works if we adopt the analogy proposed by Jeremy Waldron that was quoted above. According to Waldron, as we saw, the cheques that sometimes accompany public apologies fall into the same category as gifts that one buys for a date whom one has stood up.[13] That view seems quite right in implying that the material thing cannot plausibly be seen as an equivalent, in some odd way, of the loss or damage caused, which I think is Waldron's good point here. But flowers are clearly understood to be intended as a conventional token, whether the giver is rich or poor, while if compensation payments bore no relation to the payer's resources, they would rightly be suspected. They must represent a loss to the payer that can be taken as a measure of the payer's seriousness, even if not as a measure of what the payee lost. Only then can they be taken as a good-faith promise for the future. We can perhaps – borrowing from one theory of punishment – regard reparations as a 'penance', and hence as something that should 'take into consideration the impact on the offender'.[14] Here, though, we should note that substantial payments impose a significant burden on the whole society. The need to make them, then, is clear only in cases in which a whole society can be said to share responsibility for an atrocity, in more than the minimal sense of being citizens of it. That would be the sort of case in which there had been mass participation or else widespread support for the beliefs that the atrocity expressed.

The 'penance' view meets what may be the strongest objection to compensation, which is that it often mistakes the nature of the wrong done. As one critic has written, the idea of compensation favoured by economists assumes that the point is to restore someone (or some group) to a previous level of happiness, that what they have lost and what we can give them can be measured on a single scale, and that there is nothing particular or unique about the loss that was suffered.[15] We have seen why this is an unsatisfactory view in all three respects. Recipients are entitled to feel aggrieved by the wrong done even when compensated; monetary compensation does not provide an equivalent; and it is the particularity of the wrong that it is crucially important to recognize in processes of redress.

5. Compensation has of course been a major topic in the case of redress for African slavery. In many or even most cases, the compensation has not been directly monetary, and so escapes much of the objection that was noted just above. It has taken an 'in-kind' form, that is, the provision of opportunities that are actually meant to remedy the loss, insofar as that is possible. The Black Studies programmes introduced in universities in the United States – as at Brown University, for example, in response to revelations about its founder – are often justified as remedies for the 'cultural injustice' mentioned above: as ways to promote a sense of accomplishment and pride. Scholarships for African-Americans are intended to remedy the effects of the accumulated neglect of educational provision. Affirmative action programs in employment are intended to overcome the historic under-representation of African-Americans in better-paid sectors of the economy. Compensation of this kind can be targeted more precisely at the actual deficits suffered by a group, and so does not involve the difficult questions about what it is that cash transfers can really accomplish.

The case of slavery is especially likely to invite the thought that redress is a second-best option, given that ideas of distributive justice have lost much of their political force in the past few decades. This is the theme of a long and polemical book by the late Brian Barry, *Culture and Equality*,[16] which we might call a lament for the loss of a kind of politics in which inequality could be forthrightly attacked for what it is: Now, Barry complained, we have to look for special reasons to transfer resources to people, reasons related to group histories – we cannot respond to poverty as such, so we devise remedies for the effects of slavery. On the other hand, in contrast to a view such as Barry's, slavery is one of the prime cases for the argument made in Chapter 5, that historical redress can be distinguished from the pursuit of justice in general, because sometimes, the loss that has been suffered cannot be identified without the history. Even if, as argued

CONCLUSION

above, it is current injustice and deprivation that trigger concern about a group's circumstances, it is absurd to suppose that what can be done can somehow be figured out without reference to the group's historical experience. For a condition such as slavery, compounded by all the subsequent forms of oppression that followed formal abolition, surely has profound effects that cannot simply be equated with the effects of poverty alone.

So the issue of reparations for slavery stands at the point of intersection between two competing social theories: one, egalitarian and universalizing, proposes to put the issue on the same footing as any other form of deprivation. Injustice, it tells us, should be remedied however and whenever caused. The other, historical and contextualizing, proposes to put the issue on its own footing, as a response to unique atrocity. I see no reason why we should expect either of these theories to take up the whole moral ground, given that any event has things in common with and things that set it apart from others. And in fact, the argument of this book suggests a resolution, though of a rough-and-ready sort. In terms of current deprivation, there is both a moral and political case for treating all forms of deprivation, however caused, historical or otherwise, together, and for bringing historically oppressed minorities under the umbrella of general (i.e. not historically specific) justice. The moral case for that stems from the fact that our social categories are hopelessly approximate in terms of capturing real experience: Many members of the allegedly privileged majority have suffered deep deprivation, while some members of generally deprived minorities – those most likely to benefit from preferential treatment, as has often been noted – would likely succeed in the normal course of things. The political case is that one-issue causes face an uphill fight, and promoting one's own one issue is more likely to be effective if linked to others' one issue. So, if a progressive government had a free hand, and if minorities could form unimpeded alliances with other political actors, it would be better – for example – to work for increased funding for all schools that lacked adequate resources, rather than to demand funding for schools in racially defined ghettos.[17] (Of course I realize that the 'ifs' here are idealizing – governments do not have a free hand, and minority groups have to work with what they have. I am talking about what the argument leads to, not about what we can get right now.)

On the other hand, if we look to the future, the contextual and historically specific view has the edge, because the long-term effects of slavery or of other atrocities cannot be made good within a single generation; they call for measures that will modify the self-perception of those in the minority and the attitudes of those in the majority. Those measures, whatever they are – and this book has no magic to offer – will have to take seriously the complex ways in which the past burdens everyone. Because the effects are long-term, it seems overwhelmingly likely that remedies, whatever they are, will be intergenerational in character, and likely, then, to fit best with the general theme of this book: that our overriding concern should be to avoid transmitting the oppressive effects of the past to future generations, and that that concern best expresses the duty of *historical* redress.

6. Colonialism, the next item on the list, seems different from either the Holocaust case or the slavery case, in that for the most part those concerned do not live in close proximity, and have relations that are mediated through institutions in an impersonal way. For that reason alone, it seems to me that the right responses are going to be concrete rather than symbolic in nature, since symbolic responses seem so much more appropriate when they stand a chance of affecting the texture of relationships among people who share social space, so that a reform and refocusing of attitudes is of great or even overriding importance. It is essential, of course, that former colonial countries acknowledge and respond to particular atrocities, such as those involving Britain and Kenya, Germany and Namibia,[18] Japan and China, because it is important to maintain the standards of justice that condemn them: We need to be emphatically reminded of the need for restraints on coercive power because time and time again governments are tempted to ignore them. But as for the whole colonial experience itself? It is so integral a part of the enormous

economic and demographic changes that created the modern world that it is hard to find a vantage point from which an evaluation could be made. I can apologize to you for lying on some occasion instead of telling the truth – that is simple enough, because we know what the alternative is; but in the case of colonialism, the question would be: instead of what? ('Instead of invading others' territory' may come to mind, perhaps, but that, although simple, implies a principle that could not honestly be endorsed by many of the colonized themselves. The colonizers did not invent aggression or forcible border crossing, although they globalized it.)

Weighing the overall effects of the colonial period would of course be a gigantic task. In the brief discussion of reparations to Africa above, it was suggested that the morality of relations between first- and third-world countries should be of a forward-looking kind. The reason that was put forward was that it seems wrong to make such an important issue depend on questions about the past whose answers are contestable and perhaps even unsettlable, given the difficulty of finding a clear baseline against which to measure gains and losses. We would not want to say, surely, that everything was fine, in the economic and political relations between the first and third worlds, if our best economists told us that on some measure or other, the first world had not permanently benefited from colonialism, and that the third world was on some measure better off. If that forward-looking view seems impatient or dismissive, perhaps that is justified by the urgency of trying to respond to what is happening now. That may tip the balance away from the past-oriented territory of symbolic redress, and towards the consideration of what can be done, with practical consequences. As one political philosopher has rightly argued, redress-type arguments can be useful as a way of highlighting global injustice and motivating a response.[19] But as his account makes perfectly clear, its starting point is the fact of current injustice. Perhaps, once again, we should be cautious about being too critical of arguments whose tendency is good: but that only seems important when criticism tends to let the wealthy and powerful off the hook, and that isn't at all what is attempted here.

For over and above the specific acts of violence mentioned above, there are at least two reasons for keeping the hook in place.

To extend a point made in connection with slavery, it is an illusion to suppose that the wrong is historically very distant. Just as the formal abolition of slavery was followed by more than a century of discrimination against its victims, so too the end of colonialism can hardly be said to have brought to an end the exploitation of the colonized. Some argue, as we have seen, that the colonized, like the enslaved, internalized the inferiority implied by oppression, so that colonialism continues, as it were, within their minds. But rather than resting the argument on a deep and ambitious psychological claim of that kind, let us take a simpler and more straightforward case, one that recent debate has made familiar. After decolonization, former colonies – as sovereign nations – were entitled and often encouraged to borrow funds from private and public lenders. Many of them continue to carry a burden of debt that severely impedes their capacity to develop, and demands for debt forgiveness are prominent in global justice campaigns. What justifies these campaigns is that when a poor country borrows from first-world banks or from international institutions (the International Monetary Fund, the World Bank), the situation is rather unlike the standard borrowing scenario.[20] Those who borrow, the governing elites, have interests that are distinct from those who must repay, their citizens; and they may use the borrowed resources to increase their repressive control. New democracies are saddled with debts incurred by tyrannical predecessors. Borrowers, especially in times of crisis, have very much less bargaining power than lenders, especially as lenders are few and borrowers many. Policies and circumstances to which rich countries contribute disproportionately affect poor countries' ability to repay. Combining all this with loan conditions that often prove destructive explains why the debt burdens carried by many countries are not only unsustainable but unjustifiable in terms of fairness. It is not historical redress that is at issue, redress for things that happened long ago, but the workings of current or very recent global arrangements that are systematically unjust.

A second reason for caution about redress-type arguments, in this particular case, is that they lend themselves most readily to demands for actions that convey the idea of generosity, as a way of compensating for past selfishness: demands that we should aid now because we wronged then. This poses a twofold worry. First, the effectiveness of aid is a subject of much debate, with some opposition to it coming from people from the recipient countries themselves.[21] Second, the generosity paradigm, as we may call it, tends to distract our attention from something of greater practical importance, that is, the ways in which first-world countries sustain and profit from global institutions that impose burdens and constraints on developing countries. The list of those ways could be very long, but the philosopher Thomas Pogge, who has done more than anyone to bring this issue to light, singles out two: the effect of borrowing privileges, which, as mentioned above, enrich tyrannical governments and enable them to pass the costs on to their people, and, parallel to this, the 'resource privilege', which allows exploitative local rulers and elites to sell their country's resources to the first world without transferring much if any of the proceeds to their people.[22] To these, many have come to add, with increasing emphasis lately, the fact that rich countries create trading areas among themselves that allow protectionist policies that exclude the poorer countries from effective competition. They have also drawn attention to the damage done to the shared natural environment by the first-world countries, in the course of their development. This is one of those cases in which it is not only more realistic but also perhaps more demanding to think in terms of a 'negative' duty not to harm as opposed to a 'positive' duty to give aid.[23] Of course, we are entitled to be more generous to those with whom we identify than to outsiders; but it is a very basic moral idea that we should avoid causing harm to anyone, insider or outsider. Following up that idea to where it goes seems better than resting first-world obligations on a more speculative reparative basis.

7. Apologies were the last item on our initial list. They happened to be apologies made by churches, and they were 'pure' apologies,

in that they were not part of a larger package of measures such as compensation or restitution. Let us get the first of those aspects out of the way in order to concentrate on the second.

On a generous view, states may face all sorts of constraints in doing the right thing, including the constraint that doing one right thing might preclude doing another right thing, and also the constraint that doing the right thing may threaten their security. Since a state is a government plus people, the government's concern for the people's security amounts to another right thing that has to be thrown into the balance with the original right thing. It may or may not outweigh it. But all that seems harder to bring into play in the case of churches. States get their raison d'être from abstract values (such as civic equality) that have to be constantly reinterpreted in light of changing circumstances, so that generally speaking, in making policy, we are at one practical remove from absolute and unconditional requirements. It is probably a rare occurrence that a state can be called on to do something on the sole ground that it is right, without interpretation, and unweighed against other grounds and other priorities. But it is hard to see that we can transfer this consideration, unmodified, to churches. Of course, churches, like states, are institutions, and so, like states, have to think about issues affecting their survival in the world. But if their identity – as seems overwhelmingly likely – is more clearly connected with definite beliefs than the identity of states is, it is hard to see that their survival could justify compromising those beliefs. For what, then, would be the point of their surviving? It is probably not for a non-Catholic to comment on the claim that the church needs to compromise in order that its mission may survive in the long term. But from the standpoint of many outsiders, what seems to undermine that church today is scarcely a failure to compromise, but, rather, a willingness to temporize in order to avoid scandals, and those who share this view may feel that the apologetic tradition of John Paul II is, to put it crudely, the best bet.

CONCLUSION

Apology has an independent value, as we can see from cases in which people continue to seek them even after compensation has been given, and cases in which apology is sought without compensation. An example of the first is the infamous case of the Tuskegee experiments, in which black males were not told that they were suffering from syphilis so that they could be used as a control group. (Compensation to survivors and heirs was made in 1974, President Clinton's apology came 23 years later.) An example of the second is the Acadians' request for an apology, only, from Britain for their forcible expulsion from their lands. Another example is the suit launched in 2009 by a French citizen, K. W. Schaechter, against the national railway company for its role in transporting some 85,000 Jews to concentration camps, M. Schaechter seeking acknowledgement and damages in the symbolic amount of 1 Euro only.

A great deal has been written about the importance of apology, the main theme being its value in changing the relationship between two parties. As we saw in Chapter 3, public apologies are seen as ways for offending institutions to announce a permanent change in their behaviour towards the offended, and seen in this light, the evident dissimilarities with personal apologies are no longer surprising: Public apologies are essentially forward-looking, more equivalent to a promise than to an apology in the context of private life. But the meaning of public apologies to the recipients is somewhat different. The aspect of future security is indispensable, of course, but there is also – very often – an element of recognition. To have part of one's history ignored is a kind of affront, and when that history involves suffering at the hands of others to ignore it is to imply that the group that suffered is lacking in worth. For the same reason, ignoring or denying history implies that the offender has some sort of special lofty standing that confers impunity. So we can see an apology as a kind of levelling process. As one writer has said, 'The apology process reverses the situation by transferring the humiliation from the victims to the offenders.'[24] In this way, interestingly, it is strongly parallel to the idea of punishment discussed above, despite the fact that what it calls for is quite different.[25]

Perhaps, the classic and most long-standing case of 'denial' concerns the Turkish government's refusal to accede to the Armenians' demand for 'recognition' of what occurred in 1915, when as many as 1.5 million Armenian people died at the hands of the Turks. I will not try to go into the extraordinarily contested wrangles over whether or not the deaths amounted to genocide or, rather, to unfortunate wartime events not under the direct control of the Turkish government. I will simply say that the Armenians' tenacity in demanding recognition and apology, and, in more of a back-handed way, the Turkish government's tenacity in refusing them, amount to what is surely the best possible evidence of the importance of apology in intercommunity relations.

Of course, the Armenians' demand is not for what we have called 'pure' apology, for it is associated (at least by some Armenians) with legal demands for damages, and, more far-reachingly still, with possible political demands for a 'greater Armenia' (just as the trouble may have begun, a century ago, with dreams of a 'greater Turkey', a 'Turan' embracing all Turkic people, and excluding the ethnically and religiously different Armenian inhabitants of the area). That may explain Turkey's tenacity in refusing Armenian claims, although it may be that its tenacity owes at least as much, if not more, to a resentful sense that the (official) Turkish side of the story has not been understood. This provides an opportunity to comment, finally, on an issue that has run all the way through this book: the relation between the material aspects and what we may term the 'psychic' or symbolic aspects of redress.

That issue has come up in many ways in this book. Is material compensation something that validates an apology, or, rather, something that cheaply disguises a failure to change one's heart? Is compensation objectionable because it suggests that victims can be bought off? Is redress about getting something back, or, rather, about getting one's loss recognized? Are demands for historical redress best understood as substitutes for claims that should really be made in the

CONCLUSION

name of general equality? Are history-based claims to be accepted because they carry persuasive weight in a certain political climate, not because they carry real, persuasive moral weight? Given the variety of circumstances in which the idea of redress comes into play, there cannot be a simple answer to any of these questions. But this book has offered a line of approach to them. When wrongs have been suffered by previous generations, we need to consider the present legacy of the wrongs, and the remedy is what needs to be done in order to avoid reproducing them. That, it was argued, is how we acquire and acquit ourselves of responsibility for the acts of the past, and what underlies that responsibility is a decent concern for future generations, a concern about the injustice in their lives that they would not know about unless we tell them, in whatever is the most effective way. And there are several cases in which the good faith of that message will be undermined unless redress has a material element.

To summarize, first, there are cases in which justice can straightforwardly be done by restitution (in the literal sense) – cases, that is, in which some object can be returned without incurring further injustice, the justice and injustice of return perhaps being measured by the respective 'stakes' that are involved. Second, there are also cases in which harm to living survivors and victims' immediate relatives can be compensated, something that, it was argued, is no more problematic than the award of damages by a court. Third, there are cases where older injustices have left a long-term mark in terms of deprivation. Responding to those will be more just, and less likely to be divisive, when it is part of a general programme of correcting unjustified inequalities: It was argued above that injustices demand attention whatever their history. Fourth, there may be cases in which monetary compensation must be offered not simply to remedy harm but to acknowledge wrongdoing – when it is offered as a 'penance', something appropriate, it was suggested, when a whole society can be said to have been willingly complicit in some great injustice.

So what is left, when those four cases are accounted for? Above all, what is left is ignorance about the cruelties of the past, incomprehension of how things came to be and myths about the deservingness of history's winners. As Chapter 5 suggested, historical redress should be classed together with other devices that can help a society achieve clarity about its circumstances. Information and commemoration will be central to it. In the ways listed above, and perhaps in other ways too, redress may also have a material element – it is impossible to judge without reference to context. But the overridingly important idea that should govern modes of redress is that, as an error-prone species, we should welcome every chance to record and recover from past errors, and try to save others from them.

NOTES

Introduction

1 Including in Britain, from the beginning. In his poem *Childe Harold's Pilgrimage*, Lord Byron wrote: 'Dull is the eye that will not weep to see/Thy walls defaced, thy mouldering shrines removed/By British hands.' Recent polls suggest that public opinion in Britain still generally favours return.

2 C. Shea (2000), 'A legendary friendship', *Lingua Franca*, February, 47–55.

3 Rebecca Tsosie (2007), 'Acknowledging the past to heal the future', in Jon Miller and Rahul Kumar, eds, *Reparations: Interdisciplinary Inquiries*, Oxford: Oxford University Press, p. 49.

4 For a nuanced analysis, see Catherine Lu (2011), 'Colonialism as structural injustice: historical responsibility and contemporary redress', *Journal of Political Philosophy* 19:3, 261–81.

5 'In the world of public apologies for great historic wrongs, those articulated by John Paul II on behalf of his Church of a billion people have a special resonance, for reasons both of style and substance.' Michael Marrus (2008), 'Papal apologies of Pope John Paul II', in Mark Gibney et al., eds, *The Age of Apology: Facing Up to the Past*, Philadelphia: University of Pennsylvania Press, p. 259. Marrus quotes an Italian newspaper source that identifies 94 distinct occasions on which John Paul II apologized and/or asked for forgiveness on the Church's behalf.

6 www.politicalapologies.com

7 Aaron Lazare (2004), *On Apology*, Oxford: Oxford University Press, pp. 6–7.

8 See Jean Hampton's contributions to Jeffrie Murphy and Jean Hampton (1988), *Forgiveness and Mercy*, Cambridge: Cambridge University Press.

9 See Bernard Boxill (1972), 'The morality of reparations', *Social Theory and Practice* 2:1, 113–22.

10 For a most moving example of an act of restitution, see Edmund de Waal (2010), *The Hare with Amber Eyes*, London: Chatto and Windus.
11 Quoted in Elazar Barkan (2007), 'Reparation: a moral and political dilemma', in Miller and Kumar *Reparations*, p. 4.
12 Jeffrey Blustein (2008), *The Moral Demands of Memory*, Cambridge: Cambridge University Press, pp. 15–19.
13 See Jeremy Waldron (1992), 'Superseding historical injustice', *Ethics* 103:1, 4–28.
14 'On a three-year voyage in 1740, a British naval expedition under the command of Commodore George Anson lost fourteen hundred men out of two thousand who sailed. Four were killed by enemy action; virtually all the rest died of scurvy.' Bill Bryson (2011), *At Home: A Short History of Private Life*, New York: Doubleday, p. 165.

Chapter 1: Does the past have rights?

1 Barkan (2007), 'Reparation', in Miller and Kumar, eds, *Reparations*, p. 7.
2 Ronald Dworkin (1984), 'Rights as trumps', in Jeremy Waldron, ed., *Theories of Rights*, Oxford: Oxford University Press, p. 153.
3 See Stephen Holmes and Cass R. Sunstein (1999), *The Cost of Rights: Why Liberty Depends on Taxes*, New York: Norton.
4 Samantha Brennan (1995), suggests that it would be better to call rights 'high cards': 'How is the strength of a right determined?', *American Philosophical Quarterly* 32:4, 383–93.
5 See also Janna Thompson (2009b), 'Identity and obligation in a transgenerational polity', in Axel Gosseries and Lukas H. Meyer, eds, *Intergenerational Justice*, Oxford: Oxford University Press, p. 40.
6 Exactly this situation arises in chapter 33 of George Eliot's novel, *Romola*, in which the title character has promised her invalid father that his library of precious scholarly books will be preserved intact after his death. Romola's morally corrupt husband, Tito, sells the library at the first opportunity, and Romola says to him: 'Is it good that we should harden our hearts against all the wants and hopes of those who have depended on us? What good

can belong to men who have such souls? . . . I know of no good for cities or the world if they are to be made up of such beings.'

7 The original terms of Cecil Rhodes's Trust restricted the Scholarships to men, and an Act of the UK Parliament opened the competition to women in 1977.

8 See Paul Bahn (1984), 'Do not disturb? Archaeology and the rights of the dead', *Journal of Applied Philosophy* 1:2, 213–25.

9 Michael Ridge (2003), 'Giving the dead their due', *Ethics* 114:1, 38–59, p. 44.

10 Wilfrid Beckerman (2006), 'The Impossibility of a theory of intergenerational justice', in J. C. Tremmel, ed., *Handbook of Intergenerational Justice*, Cheltenham: Elgar.

11 An alternative theory of rights needs a mention, one according to which a right should not be understood as a particular and special kind of interest – my view – but as an entitlement to make choices, or as something that gives me the power to either insist on or to waive a duty that another person has. The dispute between 'interest' theorists and 'choice' theorists of rights is long and involved, and I bracket out the choice theory here not because I have compelling reasons to reject it, but because if it were true then the case for thinking that non-existent people (future or past ones) had rights would become impossible to sustain from the outset. On rights in general, see Peter Jones (1994), *Rights*, New York: St Martin's Press. For an attempt to reconcile the two theories, see Hillel Stener and Peter Vallentyne, 'Libertarian theories of intergenerational justice', in Gosseries and Meyer (2009).

12 Ernest Partridge (1981), 'Posthumous interests and posthumous respect', *Ethics* 91, 243–64.

13 This is simply an alternative version of a thought-experiment created by John O'Neill (2001), 'Future generations, present harms', in John O'Neill et al., eds, *Environmental Ethics and Philosophy*, Cheltenham: Elgar.

14 See, for example, Walter Glannon (2001), 'Persons, lives and posthumous harms', *Journal of Social Philosophy* 32:2, 127–42, and Stephen Winter (2010), 'Against posthumous rights', *Journal of Applied Philosophy* 27:2, 186–99.

15 See Annette Baier (1980), 'The rights of past and future persons', in Ernest Partridge, ed., *Responsibilities to Future Generations*, Buffalo: Prometheus.

16 See Daniel Sperling (2008), *Posthumous Interests: Legal and Ethical Perspectives*, Cambridge: Cambridge University Press, for an excellent review.

17 See Charles Blattberg (2009), *Patriotic Elaborations*, Montreal: McGill-Queen's University Press, chapter 3, for a vigorously engaged statement of this view.

18 Bernhard Schlink (2009), *Guilt about the Past*, Toronto: Anansi, p. 28.

Chapter 2: Who benefits?

1 Alasdair MacIntyre (1981), *After Virtue*, Notre Dame, IA: University of Notre Dame Press, p. 67.

2 Quoted in Rhoda E. Howard-Hassmann (2008), *Reparations to Africa*, Philadelphia: University of Pennsylvania Press, p. 81.

3 Ibid., p. 99.

4 See however Mathias Risse (2005), 'How does the global order harm the poor?', *Philosophy and Public Affairs* 33:4, 349–76, for a different view. The view that Risse criticizes is developed particularly by Thomas Pogge (2002), *World Poverty and Human Rights*, Cambridge: Polity.

5 Karl Marx (1977), *Capital*, vol. 1, Eng. Trans., New York: Random House, p. 915.

6 Ibid. In light of a recent work by the historian Jane Humphries (2010), we must also note the indispensable role played by the exploitation of child labour in the metropolis: *Childhood and Child Labour in the British Industrial Revolution*, Cambridge: Cambridge University Press.

7 Jared Diamond (1997), *Guns, Germs and Steel: The Fates of Human Societies*, New York: Norton.

8 David S. Landes (1998), *The Wealth and Poverty of Nations*, New York: Norton. For a balanced assessment, see Howard-Hassmann (2008), *Reparations to Africa*, chapters 6 and 7.

9 Mathias Risse (2005), 'Do we owe the global poor assistance or rectification?', *Ethics and International Affairs* 19:1, 9–18, p. 12.

10 D. Smolkin (1994), 'The non-identity problem and the appeal to future people's rights', *Southern Journal of Philosophy* 32:3, 315–19, p. 316.

NOTES

11 I think we have to extend the scope even further than Amy Sepinwall (2006), 'Responsibility for historical injustices: reconceiving the case for reparations', *Journal of Law and Politics* 22:3, 182–229, p. 183: Discussing the case of slavery, Sepinwall points out that obligations are with respect to 'any child', not to any particular child; but there would be no children of slaves had there been no slavery. Slavery is a harm to anyone affected by it, and so being a child of slaves is only one way of being someone harmed by it.

12 This argument is indebted to Rahul Kumar (2003), 'Who can be wronged?', *Philosophy and Public Affairs* 31:2, 99–118, though Kumar argues that the language of 'wronging' works better here than the language of 'harming'.

13 Robert Nozick (1974), *Anarchy, State and Utopia*, Oxford: Blackwell, pp. 93–5.

14 See Richard Arneson (1982), 'The principle of fairness and free-rider problems', *Ethics* 92:4, 616–33.

15 For the limits of this view, see Jeremy Waldron (1988), *The Right of Private Property*, Oxford: Clarendon, pp. 196–8. For its relevance to the topic of restitution, see Waldron (1992), 'Superseding historic injustice', *Ethics* 103:1, 4–28. Here we must note, however, the views of Ward Churchill (1999), who contends that we can 'never find an instance in which Indians have advocated that small property-owners be pushed off the land' and that land claims concern 'national and state parks and forests, grasslands, military reservations and the like': *Struggle for the Land*, Winnipeg: Arbeiter Ring, pp. 382–3, quoted in Burke Hendrix (2005), 'Memory in native American land claims', *Political Theory* 33:6, 763–85, p. 782. Hendrix believes that Churchill's claim is 'an overstatement' but a useful corrective.

16 See several articles by Anthony J. Sebok on the 'Findlaw' website, including 'Should claims based on African-American slavery be litigated in the courts? And if so, how?' http://writ.news.findlaw.com/sebok/20001204.html

17 This point is entirely derived from Dennis Klimchuk (2004), 'Unjust enrichment and reparations for slavery', *Boston University Law Review* 84:5, 1257–75, and from several conversations with the paper's author, for which I am most grateful.

18 Marx (1977), *Capital*, p. 271. Compare however the more familiar critique of 'wage-slavery' in *The Communist Manifesto*.

19 Loss of reputation is especially relevant to the 2007 finding by the International Court of Justice in the case of *Bosnia and Herzegovina v. Serbia and Montenegro*. Ruling that Serbia was guilty of failing to prevent genocide, the Court also ruled that the finding itself constituted satisfaction, without damages. For discussion, see Anthony Lang Jr (2011), 'Punishing genocide: a critical reading of the International Court of Justice', in Tracy Isaacs and Richard Vernon, eds, *Accountability for Collective Wrongdoing*, New York: Cambridge University Press.

20 For this view, see Jean Hampton's contributions to Murphy and Hampton (1988).

Chapter 3: What memory calls for

1 Raphael Mechoulam, quoted in Michael Pollan (2002), *The Botany of Desire*, New York: Random House, p. 160.

2 Avishai Margalit (2002), also makes this connection: *The Ethics of Memory*, Cambridge, MA: Harvard University Press, pp. 56–7.

3 John Locke (1975), *An Essay Concerning Human Understanding* [1689], Oxford: Clarendon, p. 715.

4 A diocese of the Church in Poland did this in 2010 for the remains of Copernicus.

5 For an analysis of the symbolism of the marches, see Colleen Murphy (2010), *A Moral Theory of Political Reconciliation*, New York: Cambridge University Press, pp. 10–55.

6 For an account of Afrikaner ideology, see Bruce Cauthen (1997), 'The myth of divine election and Afrikaner ethnogenesis', in Geoffrey Hosking and George Schopflin, eds, *Myths and Nationhood*, London: Hurst and Co. In his famous essay 'What is a nation?' the nineteenth-century French historian Ernest Renan proposed it as a general truth that failures rather than triumphs were basic to national memory.

7 See David Archard (1995), 'Myths, lies and historical truth: a defence of nationalism', *Political Studies* 43:3, 472–81.

8 Ibid., p. 473.

9 Ibid., pp. 479–81.

10 An (partial), exception is the South African Truth and Reconciliation Commission, for those refusing to testify or failing to testify fully were subject to criminal penalties.

NOTES

11 See Martha Minow (2000), 'The hope for healing: what truth commissions can do', in Robert I. Rotberg and Dennis Thompson, eds, *Truth and Justice*. Princeton: Princeton University Press.

12 Hannah Arendt (1963), *Eichmann in Jerusalem*, New York: Viking.

13 See David Luban (2011), 'State criminality and the ambition of international criminal law', in Isaacs and Vernon, eds, *Accountability for Collective Wrongdoing*.

14 See Isaacs and Vernon (2011), *Accountability for Collective Wrongdoing*, for a range of views.

15 Blustein (2008), *The Moral Demands of Memory*, p. 190.

16 Interestingly, the legal philosopher Larry May suggests that criminal trials, with their requirement that the defendants be given their say, may be as well or better fitted as means of getting two stories told: Larry May (2010), *Genocide: A Normative Account*, New York: Cambridge University Press, chapter 13.

17 Schlink (2009), *Guilt about the Past*, pp. 119–20. Schlink goes on to give a nuanced answer.

18 See, for example, Cillian McGrattan (2010), 'Community-based restorative justice in Northern Ireland: a neo-traditionalist paradigm?', *British Journal of Politics and International Relations* 12:3, 425–41.

19 See Rhiana Chinapen and Richard Vernon (2006), 'Justice in transition', *Canadian Journal of Political Science* 39:1, 117–34.

20 Waldron (1992), 'Superseding historical injustice', *Ethics* 103:1, 4–28, p. 5.

21 See Martha Nussbaum (1996), 'Patriotism and cosmopolitanism', in Joshua Cohen, ed., *For Love of Country*, Boston: Beacon Press.

22 Eleanor Bright Fleming (2008), 'When sorry is enough: the possibility of a national apology for slavery', in Gibney et al., eds, *The Age of Apology*, pp. 96, 106. Fleming's title refers to a widely used collection edited by Roy L. Brooks (1999), *When Sorry Isn't Enough: The Controversy over Apologies and Reparations for Human Injustice*, New York: New York University Press.

23 See Elazar Barkan (2000), *The Guilt of Nations: Restitution and Negotiating Historical Injustices*, New York: Norton, chapter 1.

24 Kathleen Gill (2000), 'The moral functions of an apology', *Philosophical Forum* 31:1, 11–27, p. 12.

25 The sincerity condition also requires, of course, that the apology not be subsequently withdrawn: 'Levi Johnston, the father of Sarah Palin's grandson, says he wishes he hadn't apologized for telling lies about the former Alaska governor because he's "never lied about anything". Johnston said in an interview on CBS's *The Early Show* on Friday that he wishes he hadn't issued the apology to Palin.' 'Johnston regrets Palin apology', *Globe and Mail* [Toronto] 28/8/2010.

26 For the view that sincerity is not always expected, see Lazare (2004), *On Apology*, p. 118. Lazare also mentions (pp. 7–8) the case of 'apology companies' in China (professionals who apologize on your behalf), and (p. 32) the view that in Japanese culture, it is the smoothing of future relations rather than sincerity that matters. Clearly there are interesting cultural differences that a full study of apologies would have to explore.

27 Janna Thompson, 'Apology, justice, and respect', in Gibney et al. (2008), *The Age of Apology*, pp. 37–8.

28 See, for example, Gill (2000), p. 20. See also Peter E. Digeser (2001), *Political Forgiveness*, Ithaca: Cornell University Press.

29 See Matt James, 'Wrestling with the past: apologies, quasi-apologies and non-apologies in Canada', in Gibney et al. (2008), *The Age of Apology*.

30 Nicholas Tavuchis (1991), *Mea Culpa: A Sociology of Apology and Reconciliation*, Stanford: Stanford University Press, p. 117.

31 Michael Cunningham (2004), 'Prisoners of the Japanese and the politics of apology: a battle over history and memory', *Journal of Contemporary History* 39:4, 561–74.

32 Waldron, 'Superseding historical injustice' (1992), p. 7.

33 See, for example, Iris Marion Young (1990), *Justice and the Politics of Difference*. Princeton: Princeton University Press, chapter 1.

34 Quoted in Gibney et al. (2008), *The Age of Apology*, p. 102.

35 Richard B. Bilder, 'The role of apology in international law', in Gibney et al. (2008), *The Age of Apology*, pp. 24–6.

Chapter 4: Because we are who we are

1 See Robert Sparrow (2000), 'History and collective responsibility', *Australasian Journal of Philosophy* 78:3, 346–59.

2 See Duncan Ivison (2000), 'Political community and historical injustice', *Australasian Journal of Philosophy* 78:3, 360–73.

NOTES

3 See Samuel Scheffler (2001), *Boundaries and Allegiances: Problems of Justice and Responsibility in Liberal Thought*, Oxford: Oxford University Press, especially chapter 6.

4 See Alan Gewirth (1988), 'Ethical universalism and particularism', *Journal of Philosophy* 85:6, 283–302, for a defence of this view.

5 See Scheffler (2001), *Boundaries and Allegiances*.

6 Alasdair MacIntyre (1995), 'Is patriotism a virtue?', in Ronald Beiner, ed., *Theorizing Citizenship*, Albany: SUNY Press, p. 224.

7 See David Miller (2004), 'Holding nations responsible', *Ethics* 11:4, 240–68.

8 See Chandran Kukathas (2003), 'Responsibility for past injustice: how to shift the burden', *Politics, Philosophy and Economics* 2, 180–93.

9 I borrow these examples from my discussion of 'Punishing collectives' in Isaacs and Vernon (2011), *Accountability for Collective Wrongdoing*.

10 See David Miller (2004), 'Holding nations responsible', *Ethics* 114:2, 240–61.

11 Blustein (2008), *The Moral Demands of Memory*, chapter 2.

12 J. M. Coetzee (2007), *Diary of a Bad Year*, New York: Penguin, p. 43.

13 See, for example, Mark Drumbl, 'Collective responsibility and postconflict justice', in Isaacs and Vernon (2011), *Accountability for Collective Wrongdoing*.

14 Janna Thompson (2009a), *Intergenerational Justice: Rights and Responsibilities in an Intergenerational Polity*, New York: Routledge, p. 1. Some interesting evidence supporting Thompson's view is provided by Michael McKenzie (1985), 'A note on motivation and future generations', *Environmental Ethics* 7:1, 63–9. This paper concerns the maintenance of large-scale irrigation systems for future generations' use.

15 An idea especially associated with the political philosopher Hannah Arendt. See, for example, Hannah Arendt (1959), *The Human Condition*, New York: Anchor, Part II.

16 Not unconditionally, though. Strong considerations about social equality support an inheritance tax.

17 See Stephen Holmes (1995), *Passions and Constraint: On the Theory of Liberal Democracy*, Chicago: University of Chicago Press, chapter 5.

18 Ibid., p. 162.

19 Janna Thompson (2000), 'Historical obligations', *Australasian Journal of Philosophy* 78:3, 334–45, p. 341.

20 Thompson (2009), *Intergenerational Justice*, pp. 82–3.

21 Ibid., p. 83.

Chapter 5: Back to the future

1 Jeff Spinner-Halev (2007), 'From historical to enduring injustice', *Political Theory* 35, 574–97.

2 Rajeev Bhargava, 'How should we respond to the cultural injustices of colonialism?', in Miller and Kumar (2007), *Reparations*, p. 216.

3 Keith Carlson (1996), 'The lynching of Louis Sam', *BC Studies* 109, 63–79.

4 Stephen Osborne (2006), 'Story of a lynching', *Geist* 60, Spring, 11–19, p. 17.

5 Gabriele Schwab (2010), *Haunting Legacies: Violent Histories and Transgenerational Trauma*, New York: Columbia University Press, gives a moving account of the survival of trauma across generations, although her examples concern the first generation only.

6 Thomas McCarthy (2004), 'Coming to terms with our past, part II: on the morality and politics of reparations for slavery', *Political Theory* 32, 750–72, pp. 764–5.

7 The principal source is Ronald Dworkin (1981), 'What is equality? Part 2', *Philosophy and Public Affairs* 10:4, 283–345.

8 John Rawls (1985), 'Justice as fairness: political not metaphysical', *Philosophy and Public Affairs* 14:3, 223–51, p. 242.

9 Richard Sennett and Jonathan Cobb (1972), *The Hidden Injuries of Class*, New York: Knopf.

10 Hannah Arendt (1967), 'Truth and politics', in Peter Laslett and W. G. Runciman, eds, *Philosophy, Politics and Society (Third Series)*, Oxford: Blackwell, pp. 106, 128.

11 See G. A. Cohen (1991), 'Capitalism, freedom and the proletariat', in David Miller ed., *Liberty*, Oxford: Oxford University Press.

12 The important difference between the two fables is that the hen's friends, the dog and the pig, actually turn down opportunities to participate, unlike the grasshopper, who is simply fey.

13 See the discussion in Brian Barry (2001), *Culture and Equality*, Cambridge MA: Harvard University Press, chapter 4.

14 Nozick (1974), *Anarchy, State and Utopia*, pp. 42–5.
15 Schlink (2009), *Guilt about the Past*, pp. 41–2.
16 The example is from David Miller (1988), 'The ethical significance of nationality', *Ethics* 98:3, 647–62, p. 655. There must, of course, be another family involved, let us call it Jones. The Joneses must have taken home the Smiths' baby. To avoid complications, let us suppose that the Jones' story is completely symmetrical with the Smiths'.

Conclusion

1 See Gary Bass (2008), *Freedom's Battle: The Origins of Humanitarian Intervention*, New York: Knopf, chapters 4–12.
2 See Kwame Anthony Appiah (2006), *Cosmopolitanism: Ethics in a World of Strangers*, New York: Norton, pp. 115–16.
3 Appiah (2006), *Cosmopolitanism*, chapter 8. Raphael Lemkin, the Polish lawyer who coined the term 'genocide', also proposed that 'vandalism' be considered an an international crime, for works of art are the property of 'civilized humanity'. Quoted in Willliam A. Schabas (2000), *Genocide in International Law*, Cambridge: Cambridge University Press, p. 26.
4 See David Lyons (1977), 'The new Indian claims and original rights to land', *Social Theory and Practice* 4:3, 249–72.
5 Waldron, 'Superseding historical injustice' (1992). See also the same author's 'Why is indigeneity important?', in Miller and Kumar (2007), *Reparations*.
6 Burke A. Hendrix (2010), 'Political theorists as dangerous social actors', *Critical Review of International Social and Political Philosophy* 13, first published 11 November (first).
7 James Tully (1995), *Strange Multiplicity: Constitutionalism in an Age of Diversity*, Cambridge: Cambridge University Press.
8 Michael Freeman (2002), 'Past wrongs and liberal justice', *Ethical Theory and Moral Practice* 5:2, 201–20, pp. 212–14.
9 Tamar Meisels (2003), 'Can corrective justice ground claims to territory?', *Journal of Political Philosophy* 11:1, 65–88, p. 69.
10 The Canadian experience is given a moving and informative treatment in a novel by James Bartleman (2011), *As Long as the Rivers Flow*, Toronto:

Knopf Canada. The author was the first native Lieutenant-Governor of the Province of Ontario.

11 Quoted in Barkan (2000), *The Guilt of Nations*, p. 27.
12 The story is told in Barkan (2000), *The Guilt of Nations*, chapter 1.
13 Waldron, 'Superseding historical injustice' (1992), p. 7.
14 Christopher Bennett (2008), *The Apology Ritual: A Philosophical Theory of Punishment*, Cambridge: Cambridge University Press, p. 178.
15 Debra Satz, 'Countering the wrongs of the past: the role of compensation', in Miller and Kumar (2007), *Reparations*, p. 179.
16 Barry (2001), *Culture and Equality*.
17 See ibid., chapter 6.
18 For an account of this (less familiar) issue, see Leonard Jamfa, 'Germany faces colonial history in Namibia: a very ambiguous "I am sorry"', in Gibney et al. (2008), *The Age of Apology*.
19 Kok-Chor Tan, 'Colonialism, reparations, and global justice', in Miller and Kumar (2007), *Reparations*.
20 This paragraph draws on Christian Barry and Lydia Tomitova (2007), 'Fairness in sovereign debt', in Christian Barry et al., eds, *Dealing Fairly with Developing Country Debt*, Malden, MA: Blackwell.
21 Dambisa Moyo's 2009 book *Dead Aid* (New York: Farrar Straus Giroux) is an example, though a controversial one. Her many critics complain that the book overlooks the successes of some aid projects.
22 Thomas Pogge (2002), *World Poverty and Human Rights*, pp. 112–16.
23 Thomas Pogge (2002), 'Cosmopolitanism: a defence', *Critical Review of International Social and Political Philosophy* 5:3, 86–91.
24 Lazare (2004), *On Apology*, p. 52.
25 For an extended account of the connection between apology and punishment, see Bennett (2008), *The Apology Ritual*.

BIBLIOGRAPHY

Anon. (2010) 'Johnston regrets Palin apology', *Globe and Mail* [Toronto] 28 August.
Appiah, K. A. (2006) *Cosmopolitanism: Ethics in a World of Strangers*. New York: Norton.
Archard, D. (1995) 'Myths, lies and historical truth: a defence of nationalism', *Political Studies* 43:3, 472–81.
Arendt, H. (1959) *The Human Condition*. New York: Anchor.
—. (1963) *Eichmann in Jerusalem*. New York: Viking.
—. (1967) 'Truth and politics', in P. Laslett and W. G. Runciman (eds), *Philosophy, Politics and Society (Third Series)*. Oxford: Blackwell, pp. 104–33.
Arneson, R. (1982) 'The principle of fairness and free-rider problems', *Ethics* 92:4, 616–33.
Bahn, P. (1984) 'Do not disturb? Archaeology and the rights of the dead', *Journal of Applied Philosophy* 1:2, 213–25.
Baier, A. (1980) 'The rights of past and future persons', in E. Partridge (ed.), *Responsibilities to Future Generations*. Buffalo: Prometheus, pp. 171–86.
Barkan, E. (2000) *The Guilt of Nations: Restitution and Negotiating Historical Injustices*. New York: Norton.
Barry, B. (2001) *Culture and Equality*. Cambridge, MA: Harvard University Press.
Barry, C. and L. Tomitova (2007) 'Fairness in sovereign debt', in C. Barry, B. Herman and L. Tomitova (eds), *Dealing Fairly with Developing Country Debt*. Malden, MA: Blackwell, pp. 41–79.
Bartleman, J. (2011) *As Long as the Rivers Flow*. Toronto: Knopf Canada.
Bass, G. (2008) *Freedom's Battle: The Origins of Humanitarian Intervention*. New York: Knopf.
Beckerman, W. (2006) 'The impossibility of a theory of intergenerational justice', in J. C. Tremmel (ed.), *Handbook of Intergenerational Justice*. Cheltenham: Elgar, pp. 53–71.
Bennett, C. (2008) *The Apology Ritual: A Philosophical Theory of Punishment*. Cambridge: Cambridge University Press.

Blatttberg, C. (2009) *Patriotic Elaborations*. Montreal: McGill-Queen's University Press.

Blustein, J. (2008) *The Moral Demands of Memory*. Cambridge: Cambridge University Press.

Boxill, B. (1972) 'The morality of reparations', *Social Theory and Practice* 2:1, 113–22.

Brennan, S. (1995) 'How is the strength of a right determined?' *American Philosophical Quarterly* 32:4, 383–93.

Brooks, R. L. (1999) *When Sorry Isn't Enough: The Controversy over Apologies and Reparations for Human Injustice*. New York: New York University Press.

Bryson, B. (2010) *At Home: A Short History of Private Life*. New York: Doubleday.

Carlson, K. (1996) 'The lynching of Louis Sam', *BC Studies* 109, 63–79.

Cauthen, B. (1997) 'The myth of divine election and Afrikaner ethnogenesis', in G. Hosking and G. Schopflin (eds), *Myths and Nationhood*. London: Hurst and Co., pp. 107–31.

Chinapen, R. and R. Vernon (2006) 'Justice in transition', *Canadian Journal of Political Science* 39:1, 117–34.

Coetzee, J. M. (2007) *Diary of a Bad Year*. New York: Penguin.

Cohen, G. A. (1991) 'Capitalism, freedom and the proletariat', in David Miller (ed.), *Liberty*. Oxford: Oxford University Press, pp. 163–82.

Cunningham, M. (2004) 'Prisoners of the Japanese and the politics of apology: a battle over history and memory', *Journal of Contemporary History* 39:4, 561–74.

De Waal, E. (2010) *The Hare with Amber Eyes*. London: Chatto and Windus.

Diamond, J. (1997) *Guns, Germs and Steel: The Fates of Human Societies*. New York: Norton.

Digeser, P. E. (2001) *Political Forgiveness*. Ithaca: Cornell University Press.

Dworkin, R. (1981) 'What is equality? Part 2: equality of resources', *Philosophy and Public Affairs* 10:4, 283–345.

— (1984) 'Rights as trumps', in J. Waldron (ed.), *Theories of Rights*. Oxford: Oxford University Press, pp. 153–67.

Eliot, G. (1994) *Romola*. Oxford: Oxford University Press.

Freeman, M. (2002) 'Past wrongs and liberal justice', *Ethical Theory and Moral Practice* 5:2, 201–20.

Gewirth, A. (1988) 'Ethical universalism and particularism', *The Journal of Philosophy* 85:6, 283–302.

Gibney, M., R. Howard-Hassmann, J.-M. Coicaud and N. Steiner (2008) *The Age of Apology: Facing Up to the Past*. Philadelphia: University of Pennsylvania Press.

BIBLIOGRAPHY

Gill, K. (2000) 'The moral functions of an apology', *Philosophical Forum* 31:1, 11–27.

Glannon, W. (2001) 'Persons, lives and posthumous harms', *Journal of Social Philosophy* 32:2, 127–42,

Hendrix, B. (2005) 'Memory in native American land claims', *Political Theory* 33:6, 763–85.

—. (2010) 'Political theorists as dangerous social actors', *Critical Review of International Social and Political Philosophy* 13, first published 11 November.

Hillerman, T. (1991) *Talking God*. New York: Harper Collins.

Hobbes, T. (1994) *Leviathan*. Indianapolis: Hackett.

Holmes, S. (1995) *Passions and Constraint: On the Theory of Liberal Democracy*. Chicago: University of Chicago Press.

Holmes, S. and C. R. Sunstein (1999) *The Cost of Rights: Why Liberty Depends on Taxes*. New York: Norton.

Howard-Hassmann, R. E. (2008) *Reparations to Africa*. Philadelphia: University of Pennsylvania Press.

Humphries, J. (2010) *Childhood and Child Labour in the British Industrial Revolution*. Cambridge: Cambridge University Press.

Isaacs, T. and R. Vernon (eds) (2011) *Accountability for Collective Wrongdoing*. New York: Cambridge University Press.

Ivison, D. (2000) 'Political community and historical injustice', *Australasian Journal of Philosophy* 78:3, 360–73.

James, P. D. (1992) *The Children of Men*. Harmondsworth: Penguin.

Jones, P. (1994) *Rights*. New York: St Martin's Press.

Klimchuk, D. (2004) 'Unjust enrichment and reparations for slavery', *Boston University Law Review* 84:5, 1257–75.

Kukathas, C. (2003) 'Responsibility for past injustice: how to shift the burden', *Politics, Philosophy and Economics* 2:2, 180–93.

Kumar, R. (2003) 'Who can be wronged?' *Philosophy and Public Affairs* 31:2, 99–118.

Landes, D. S. (1998) *The Wealth and Poverty of Nations*. New York: Norton.

Lazare, A. (2004) *On Apology*. Oxford: Oxford University Press.

Locke, J. (1975) *An Essay Concerning Human Understanding* [1689]. Oxford: Clarendon.

Lu, C. (2011) 'Colonialism as structural injustice: historical responsibility and contemporary redress', *Journal of Political Philosophy* 19:3, 261–81.

Lyons, D. (1977) 'The new Indian claims and original rights to land', *Social Theory and Practice* 4:3, 249–72.

MacIntyre, A. (1981) *After Virtue*. Notre Dame, IA: University of Notre Dame Press.

—. (1995) 'Is patriotism a virtue?', in Ronald Beiner (ed.), *Theorizing Citizenship*. Albany: SUNY Press, pp. 209–28.

Margalit, A. (2002) *The Ethics of Memory*. Cambridge, MA: Harvard University Press.

Marx, K. (1977) *Capital*, vol. 1. Eng. trans. New York: Vintage.

Marx, K. and F. Engels (1992) *The Communist Manifesto*. Oxford: Oxford University Press.

May, L. (2010) *Genocide: A Normative Account*. New York: Cambridge University Press.

McCarthy, T. (2004) 'Coming to terms with our past, Part II: on the morality and politics of reparations for slavery', *Political Theory* 32:6, 750–72.

McGrattan, C. (2010) 'Community-based restorative justice in Northern Ireland: a neo-traditionalist paradigm?' *British Journal of Politics and International Relations* 12:3, 425–41.

McKenzie, M. (1985) 'A note on motivation and future generations', *Environmental Ethics* 7:1, 63–9.

Meisels, T. (2003) 'Can corrective justice ground claims to territory?' *Journal of Political Philosophy* 11:1, 65–88.

Mill, J. S. (1991) *On Liberty and Other Essays*. Oxford: Oxford University Press.

Miller, D. (1988) 'The ethical significance of nationality', *Ethics* 98:3, 647–62.

—. (2004) 'Holding nations responsible', *Ethics* 114:2, 240–68.

Miller, J. and R. Kumar (eds) (2007) *Reparations: Interdisciplinary Inquiries*. Oxford: Oxford University Press.

Minow, M. (2000) 'The hope for healing: what can truth commissions do?', in R. I. Rotberg and D. Thompson (eds), *Truth and Justice*. Princeton: Princeton University Press, pp. 235–60.

Moyo, D. (2009) *Dead Aid*. New York: Farrar Straus Giroux.

Murphy, C. (2010) *A Moral Theory of Political Reconciliation*. New York: Cambridge University Press.

Murphy, J. and J. Hampton (1988) *Forgiveness and Mercy*. Cambridge: Cambridge University Press.

Nozick, R. (1974) *Anarchy, State and Utopia*. Oxford: Blackwell.

O'Neill, J. (2001) 'Future generations, present harms', in J. O'Neill, R. Turner and I. Bateman (eds), *Environmental Ethics and Philosophy*. Cheltenham: Elgar, pp. 181–97.

Osborne, S. (2006) 'Story of a lynching', *Geist* 60, Spring, 11–19.

Partridge, E. (1981) 'Posthumous interests and posthumous respect', *Ethics* 91:2, 243–64.

Pascal, B. (1966) *Pensées*, Eng. trans. Harmondsworth: Penguin.

Plato (1961) *The Collected Dialogues*, E. Hamilton and H. Cairns (eds). Princeton: Princeton University Press.

Pogge, T. (2002a) 'Cosmopolitanism: a defence', *Critical Review of International Social and Political Philosophy* 5:3, 86–91.

—. (2002b) *World Poverty and Human Rights*. Cambridge: Polity.

Political apologies website, www.politicalapologies.com

Pollan, M. (2002) *The Botany of Desire*. New York: Random House, p. 160.

Rawls, J. (1985) 'Justice as fairness: political not metaphysical', *Philosophy and Public Affairs* 14:3, 223–51.

Renan, E. (1996) 'What is a nation?', in G. Eley and R. G. Suny, *Becoming National: A Reader*. New York: Oxford University Press, pp. 41–55.

Ridge, M. (2003) 'Giving the dead their due', *Ethics* 114:1, 38–59.

Risse, M. (2005a) 'Do we owe the global poor assistance or rectification?' *Ethics and International Affairs* 19:1, 9–18.

—. (2005b) 'How does the global order harm the poor?' *Philosophy and Public Affairs* 33:4, 349–76.

Schabas, W. (2000) *Genocide in International Law*. Cambridge: Cambridge University Press.

Scheffler, S. (2001) *Boundaries and Allegiances: Problems of Justice and Responsibility in Liberal Thought*. Oxford: Oxford University Press.

Schlink, B. (2009) *Guilt about the Past*. Toronto: Anansi.

Schwab, G. (2010) *Haunting Legacies: Violent Histories and Transgenerational Trauma*. New York: Columbia University Press.

Sebok, A. J. (2000) 'Should claims based on African-American slavery be litigated in the courts? And if so, how?' http://writ.news.findlaw.com/sebok/20001204.html

Sennett, R. and J. Cobb (eds) (1972) *The Hidden Injuries of Class*. New York: Knopf.

Sepinwall, A. (2006) 'Responsibility for historical injustices: reconceiving the case for reparations', *Journal of Law and Politics* 22:3, 182–229.

Shea, C. (2000) 'A legendary friendship', *Lingua Franca*, February, 47–55.

Smolkin, D. (1994) 'The non-identity problem and the appeal to future people's rights', *Southern Journal of Philosophy* 32:3, 315–29.

Sparrow, R. (2000) 'History and collective responsibility', *Australasian Journal of Philosophy* 78:3, 346–59.

Sperling, D. (2008) *Posthumous Interests: Legal and Ethical Perspectives*. Cambridge: Cambridge University Press.

Spinner-Halev, J. (2007) 'From historical to enduring injustice', *Political Theory* 35:5, 574–97.

Tavuchis, N. (1999) *Mea Culpa: A Sociology of Apology and Reconciliation*. Stanford: Stanford University Press.

Thompson, J. (2000) 'Historical obligations', *Australasian Journal of Philosophy* 78:3, 334–45.

—. (2009a) *Intergenerational Justice: Rights and Responsibilities in an Intergenerational Polity*. New York: Routledge.

—. (2009b) 'Identity and obligation in a transgenerational polity', in Axel Gosseries and Lukas H. Meyer, eds, *Intergenerational Justice*. Oxford: Oxford University Press, p. 40.

Tully, J. (1995) *Strange Multiplicity: Constitutionalism in an Age of Diversity*. Cambridge: Cambridge University Press.

Vernon, R. (2010) *Cosmopolitan Regard: Political Membership and Global Justice*. Cambridge: Cambridge University Press.

Waldron, J. (1988) *The Right of Private Property*. Oxford: Clarendon.

—. (1992) 'Superseding historical injustice', *Ethics* 103:1, 4–28.

Weber, M. (1958) *The Protestant Ethic and the Spirit of Capitalism*. Eng. trans. New York: Scribner.

Winter, S. (2010) 'Against posthumous rights', *Journal of Applied Philosophy* 27:2, 186–99.

Young, I. M. (1990) *Justice and the Politics of Difference*. Princeton: Princeton University Press.

INDEX

aboriginal people-land claims 1
   artefacts 1, 10, 134
   residential schools 2, 18,
     139–40
   sovereignty of 137
   treaties with 107–10
Abu Ghraib 101
Acadians, expulsion of 4, 151
Aetna Insurance 3, 57
affirmative action 25, 28, 118, 125
Africa, reparations for 45–6, 147
Afrikaners 4, 70, 77–8
aid, effectiveness of 149
ants and grasshoppers 122
Apartheid 77
apologies 151–2
   and cash payments 83
   and compensation 152–4
   conditions for 81
   currency of 5
   and identity 86–7
   personal and political 81, 86,
     151
   politics of 82–3
   public and private 151
   sincerity test 81–2
Appiah, K. A. 133
archaeology 23–4
Arendt, H. 75, 120n. 10

Armenian genocide 3, 152–3
art, return of 1, 18, 133
Arthur, King 70
atrocity and crime 74
Auschwitz 76

Barry, B. 141
baseline problems in
   measurement 47–52
Bell, G. (Bishop) 97–8
benefits, compared with rights 40
   limits of argument from 41–2, 63
Beothuk people 12
Bhargava, R. 114
Blustein, J. 100
Borges, J. 65
Boyne, battle of 68, 69–70
Brown University 3, 144

Carlson, K. 115
Cherokee people 135
choices and circumstances 117–18
churches 149–50
Civil War (US) 113
claimants, multiplicity of 108–9
clarity, right to 122–30, 152
class, social 120–1
Clinton, B. (President) 82
Coetzee, J. M. 101

cold cases 34–5
colonialism 8, 11, 41, 51, 146–7
'comfort women' 2, 17–18, 141
compensation, defined 7
 and distributive justice 84–5
 purpose of 141–4
 as token 83
complicity in state action 102–4, 111, 131
consent 103
constitutions, endurance of 106–7
continuity of victims and oppressors 11
conventional duties, changes in 91–2
Cromwell, O. 111, 113
cultural injustice 114

Darwin, C. 4
death, moment of 33–4
debt forgiveness 148
deceased people, interests of 24–30
 harm to 30–2
Dickens, C. 27
dispossession, as permanent basis for challenge 124
distributive justice 85, 117, 130, 144
Dresden, bombing of 88
Drogheda, siege of 9, 111, 113
Dunkirk evacuation 70–1

economists, and mean people 53
Eichmann, A., trial of 75
Eisenhower, D. (General and President) 98
Elgin (Parthenon) Marbles 1, 7, 132–4
'Elginism' 132
Eliot, G. 23n. 6

ends and means 98–100
endurance of injustice 112–14
endurance of wrongs 110
Epicurus 34
equality 63
 language of 120
 of opportunity 117
Europe, natural advantages of 46
experience machine, idea of 127

facts, historical 120–1
Falklands War 111
Felicia's Journey (novel and film) 100
free-riding 53

Galileo 4
generalization, capacity for 37
Ghana 133
global justice 48
good samaritanism 55
groups, accountability of 99–101
guilt, transmission of 41

Hillerman, T. 132
Hiroshima 32
Hitler, attempted assassination of 98
Hobbes, T. 103
Holocaust 2, 18, 38, 76, 141, 149
 German reparations for 80–1
Huguenots 9
Human Rights, Universal Declaration of 37

identity, issue of 48–50
 and interpretation 89
 and relationships 90–1
 see also nation, continuity of; states, contrasted with nations

INDEX

immigrants, responsibility of 43
inequality *see* equality
inheritance 54
injustice, and intervening
    events 10
  global 13
  old and recent 110
  present deprivation view of 8,
    14, 112, 116, 137, 145
interests, two kinds of 28–30
  harm to 32
international criminal tribunals 62,
  141
International Monetary Fund 148
internments in wartime 2, 140
Israel-Palestine 77

James, P. D. 105
Japanese-Americans and
    Japanese-Canadians 2,
    84 *see also* internments in
    wartime
Jefferson, T. 107
Jenkins's Ear, war of 115

Kenyan 'emergency' 4, 17, 141,
  146

land, value of 135–6
Lebanon 78
life, description of 30–2
Little Red Hen (fable) 123
Locke, J. 65
Louis XIV 41

McCarthy, J. (Senator) 98
majority privilege 124–5
Marx, K., on slavery 46
  on wage labour 60
memory, surfeit of 8
  apparatus of 66

  construction of 73–5
  and discovery 68–9
  and history 67–8
  personal and political 72
  and rehearsal of past 69–70
  and responsibility 64–6
  types of 67–72
Mill, J. S. 124–5
Miller, D. 99n.10, 127–8
moral education 79–80
moral practice 23, 106
moral standards, change in 10,
  135–6
multiculturalism 5
murder, rights and 33
museum 67, 134
myth 69, 71, 130, 154

Nanking massacre 17
narratives 77–9
nation, continuity of 95–7
  distinguished from state 94–5,
    102
  national values and
    commitments 97–9
'National Sorry Day' (Australia) 85
Nelson, H. (Lord) 109
Nietzsche, F. 65
Northern Ireland 68, 78
Nozick, R. 52–3, 132

'ought implies can', principle of 54
Oxfam 37

Pascal, B. 83–4
penance theory of
  punishment 143
Pennier, C. (Grand Chief) 115
Plato 43, 52
Pogge, T. 149
political entrepreneurs 12, 109

Portugal 42
posthumous desires 22–4
potato famine (Ireland) 113
professional ethics 93, 95–7
promises, deathbed 23
property, theory of 55–6
  ideas of 136
protectionism 149
Protestantism 46
psychotherapy 101
public debt 106–7
public goods 53, 107
punishment 5, 152
  as response to unfairness 62–3, 74

Quebec 95

Racism, World Congress against (2001) 8
Rawls, J. 119n. 8
redress, three forms of 7
  culture of 84
refugees 15, 109
Reid, B. (artist) 138
remains, human 10, 134
reproduction of injustice 112, 130, 131, 140, 146
responsibility, of present generations 15, 16, 41
restitution, defined 7
'revealing is healing' 73
Rhodes, C. and Rhodes Scholarships 61–2
Riel Rebellion 9
rights 18
  and choice 27
  claimed by proxy 27–8
  critics of 36–7
  of deceased 25
  of future people 122–6, 131–2
  interests and 21, 25–6
  and moral currency 135
  posthumous 32
  tests for 128–9
  as trumps 20
  value of 19, 21, 126
  violations of 35–6
  and vulnerability 38–9
Romeo and Juliet 92–3
Romulus and Remus 69, 71
Rwanda 15, 62

sailors, in eighteenth century 12, 109
St Louis, (Ship) 115
Sam, L. (lynching victim) 114–16
Schaechter, K. W. 151
Schlink, B. 38, 76–7, 127
sense of efficacy 119
Serbs 70
slavery, restitution for 3, 24–6, 109
  benefits retained from 44–7, 51
Smithsonian Institution 1
Socrates 52
Soros, G. 16
South Africa, apology to 4
sport 89
stakes argument 134
states, contrasted with nations 102
  intergenerational nature of 104–8
  terror and 103
Sto:lo people 114–15
Swiss banks 3

'that was then' 8, 61
Thompson, J. 82, 104
treaties, endurance of 107–8
Truman Show (film) 127

INDEX

truth, varieties of 68–73, 140
Truth and Reconciliation
    Commissions 72
  Canada 76–7
  South Africa 73
truth commissions 2, 140
  and liberal-democracy 74, 75–6
  and trials 74, 78, 140
Tuskegee experiments 151

Unjust Enrichment, law of 44,
    56–61, 80
  ethical point of 59–60
  and fault 56–7
  and slavery 57–60

Valkyrie (film) 98
vengeance 92–3
Versailles, Treaty of 142

Waldron, J. 79, 83n. 32, 136, 143
Wallace, G. (Governor) 100
war debts 142
Weber, M. 46
wills 21–3
World Bank 148
World Vision 37

Zeno 33–4
Zionism 138